Enjoy !

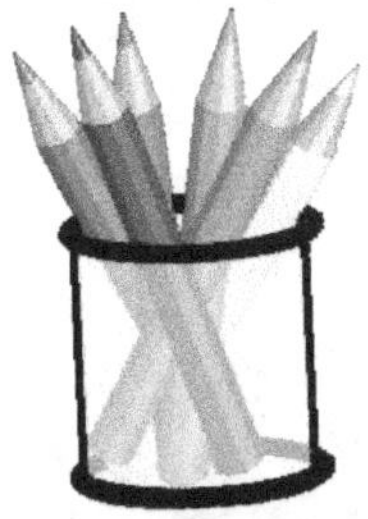

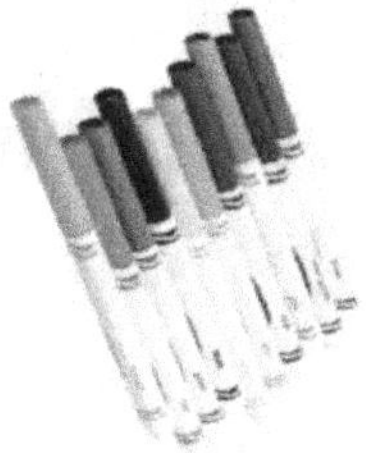

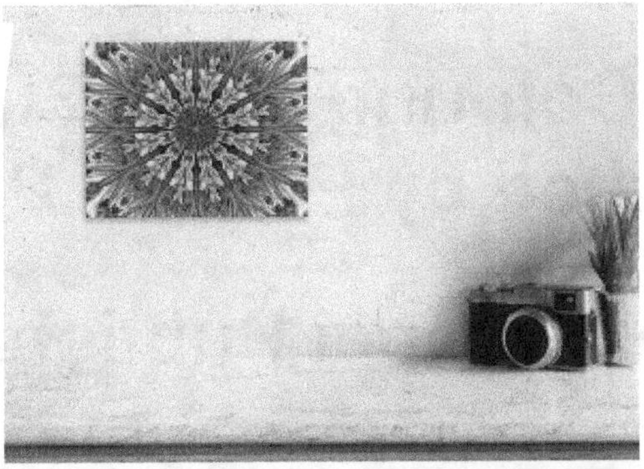

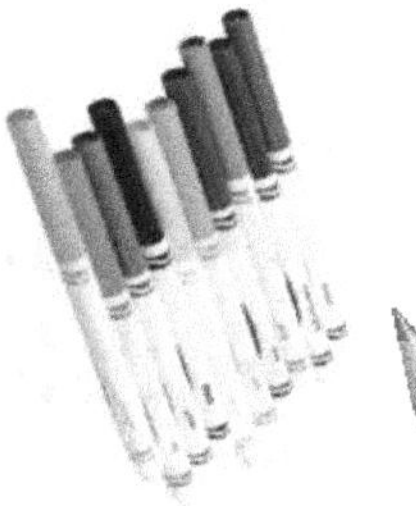

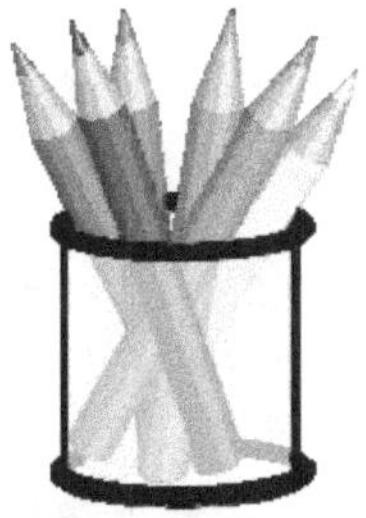

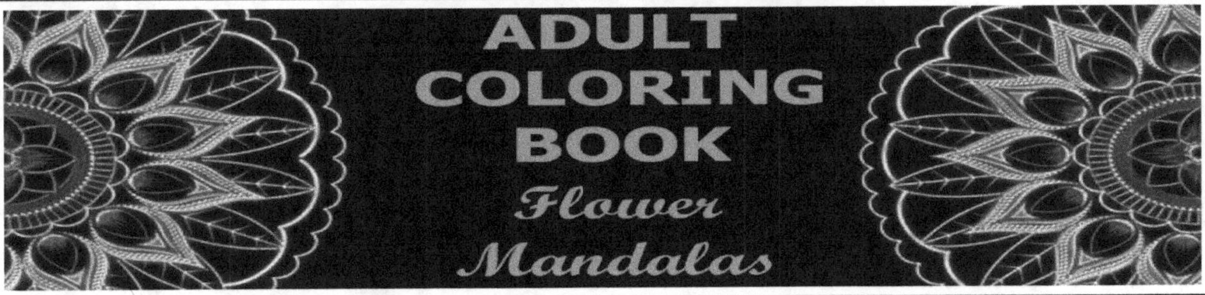

ADULT COLORING BOOK Flower Mandalas

Adult Coloring Book Flower Mandalas

Will Create Relaxation and Stress Relief.

This Is An Adult Coloring Boo k That Will Fo rce You To Relax And Focus, With A Clear And Positive Mind.

The Vision Of Color Can Help Relieve Anxiety And Depression.

Enjoy Coloring … And Then Being The Best You Want To Be !

55 Mandala Images   Are Printed O n The Fro nt Pages Only, So You Don't Need To Worry About Ink Bl eed-Through, If You Choose To Use Markers.

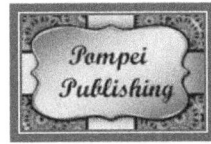

Pompei Publishing

Adult Coloring Book Flower Mandalas
Published by Pompei Publishing

© 2019 Pompei Publishing

Cover by Pompei Publishing

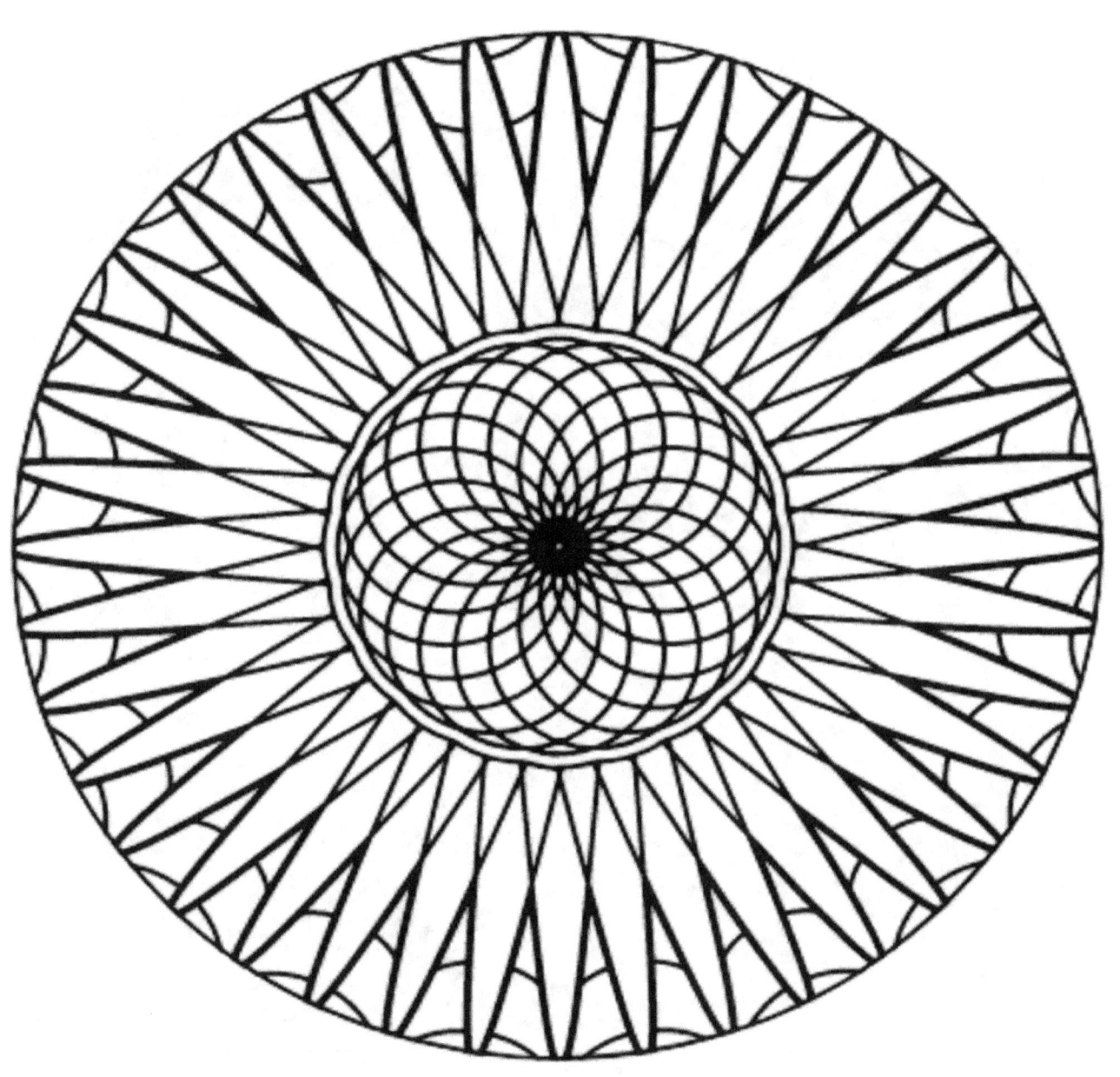

BLANK

PAGE

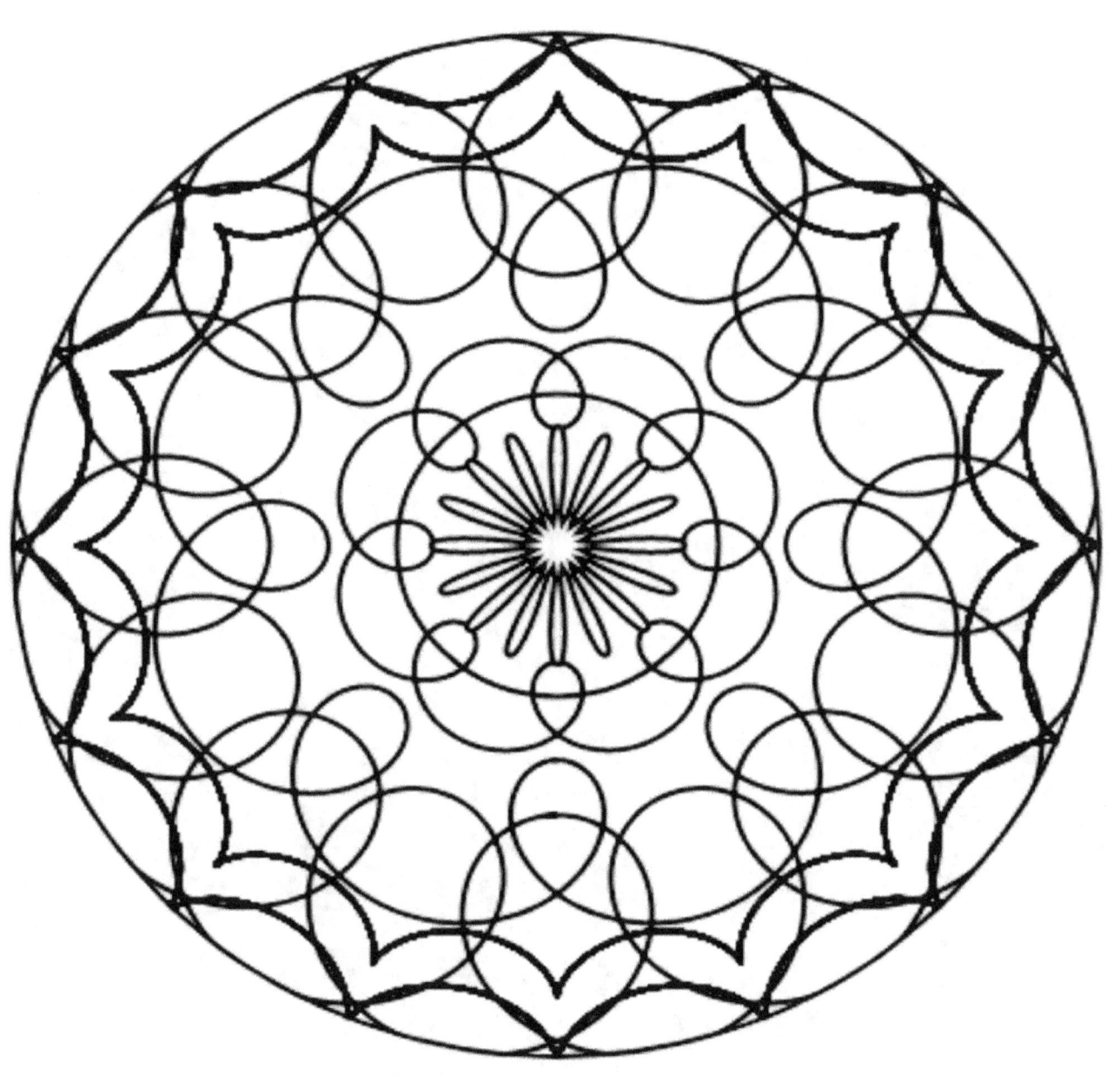

BLANK

PAGE

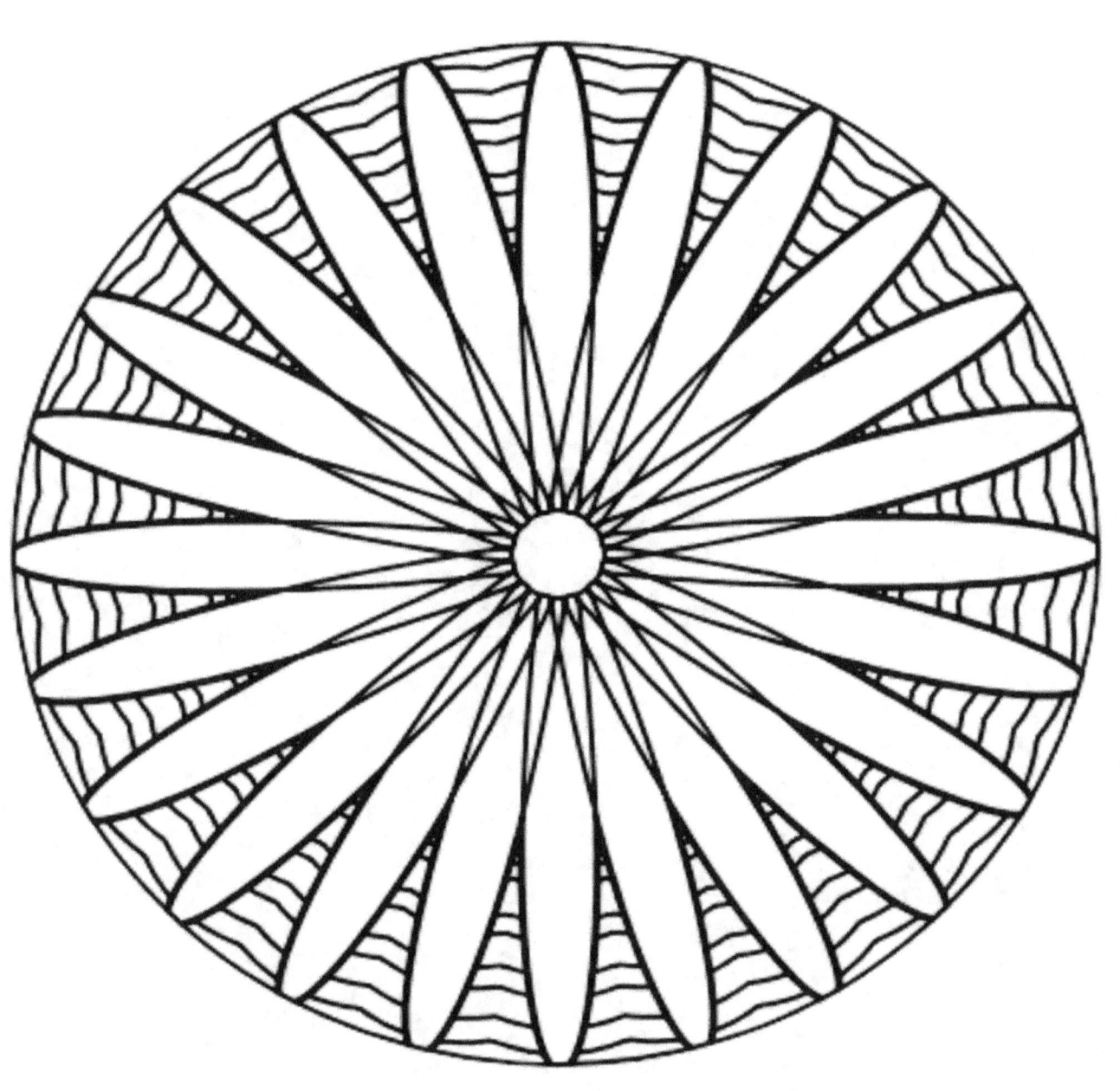

BLANK

PAGE

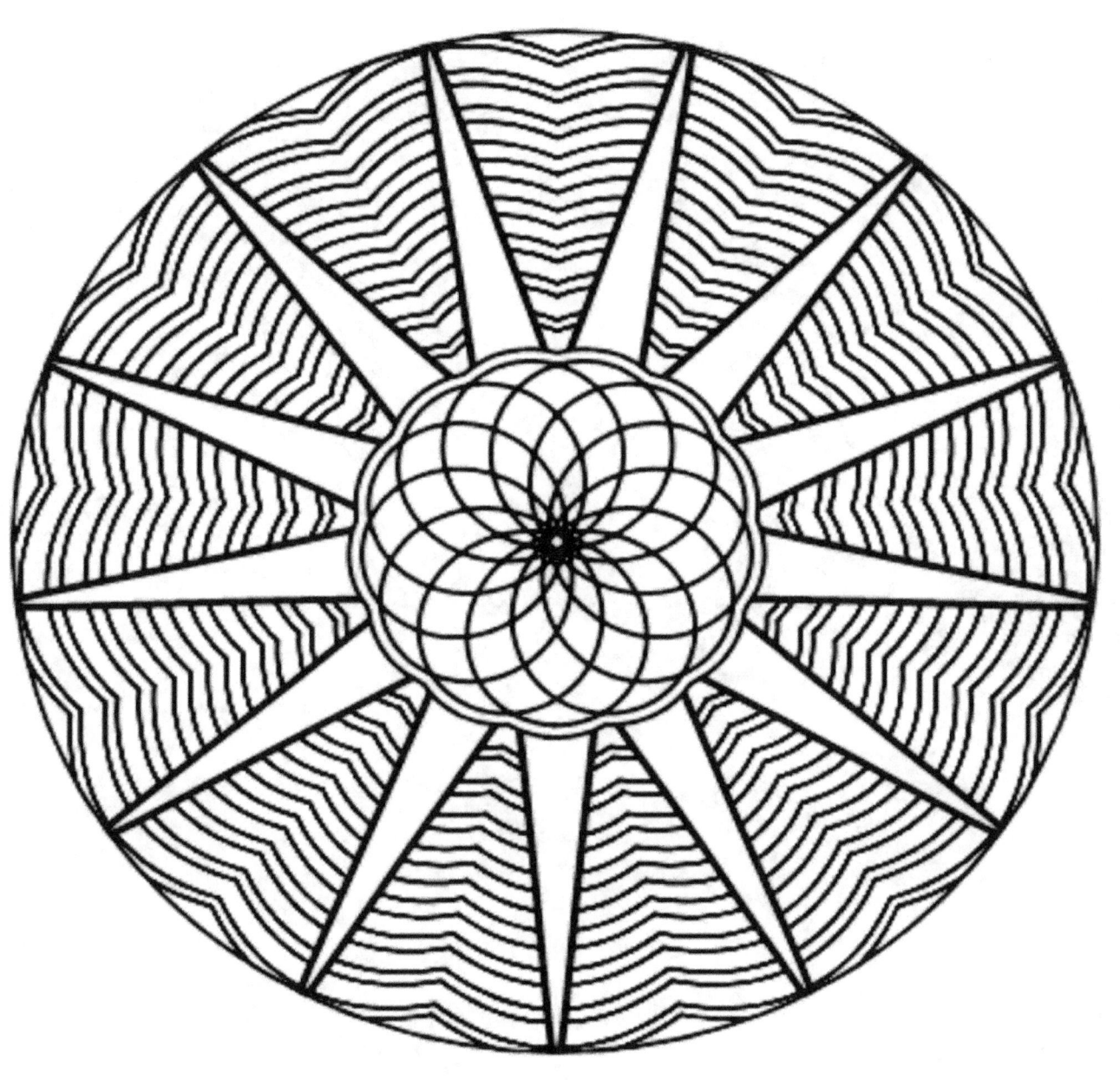

BLANK

PAGE

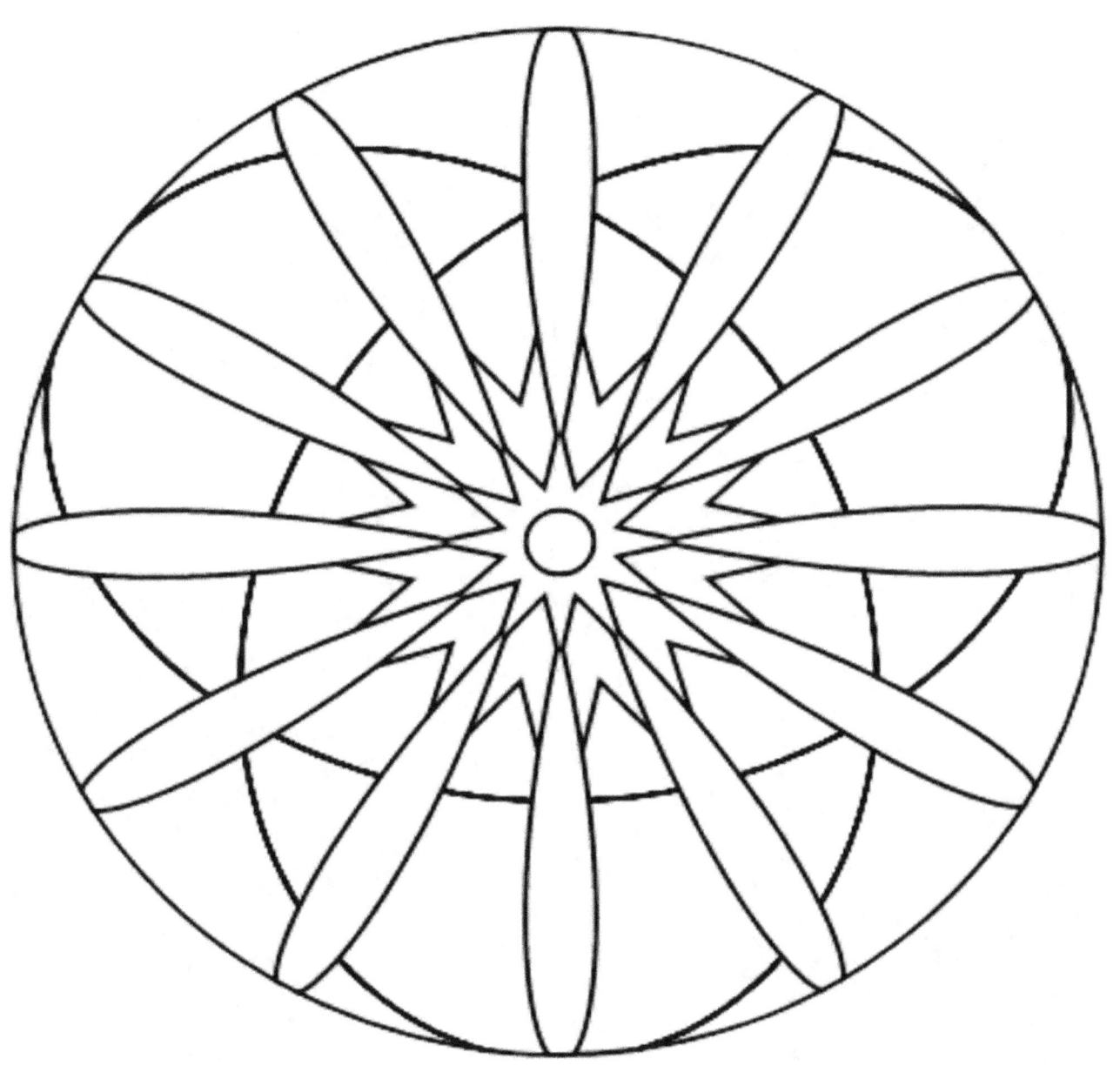

BLANK

PAGE

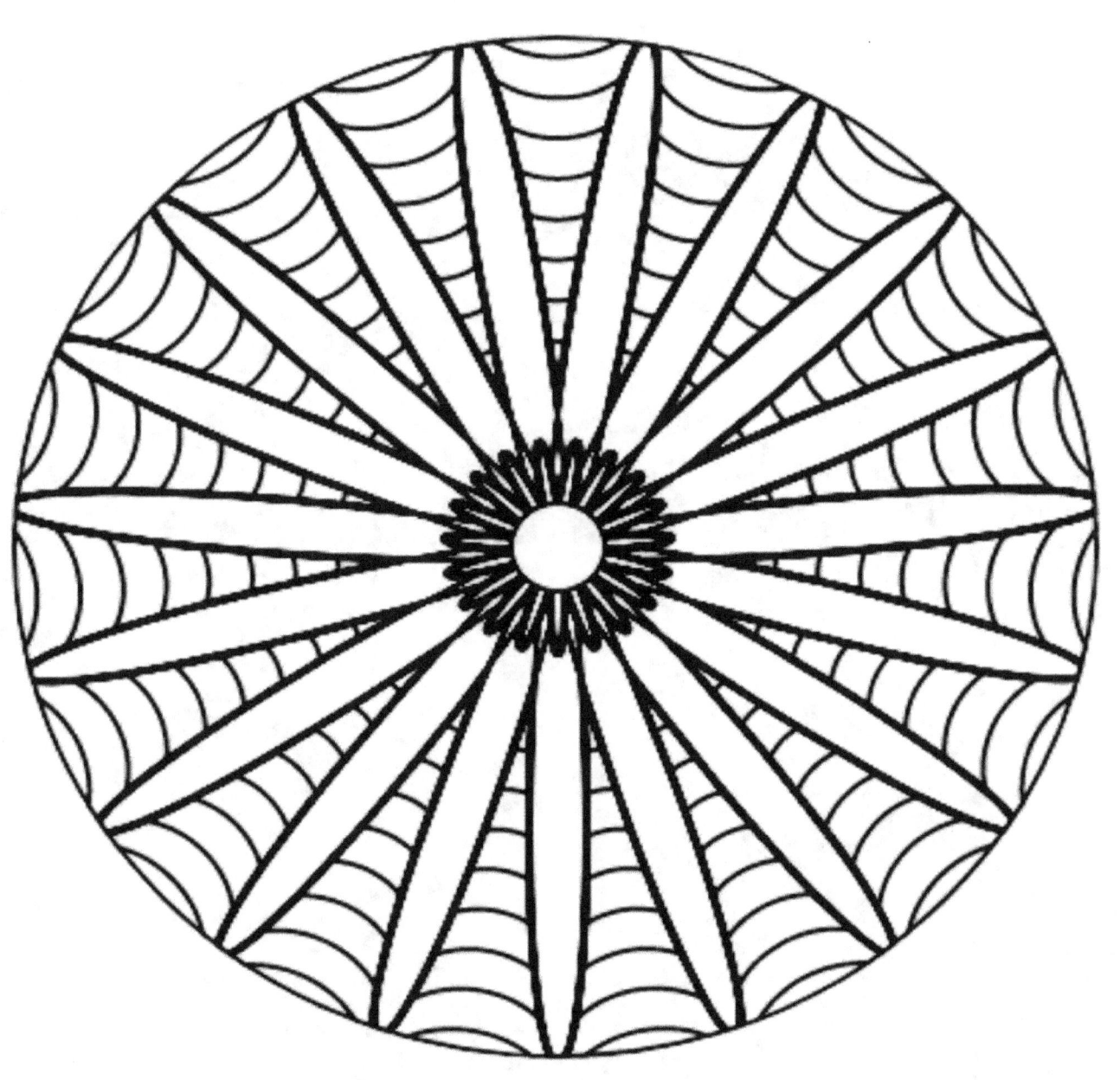

BLANK

PAGE

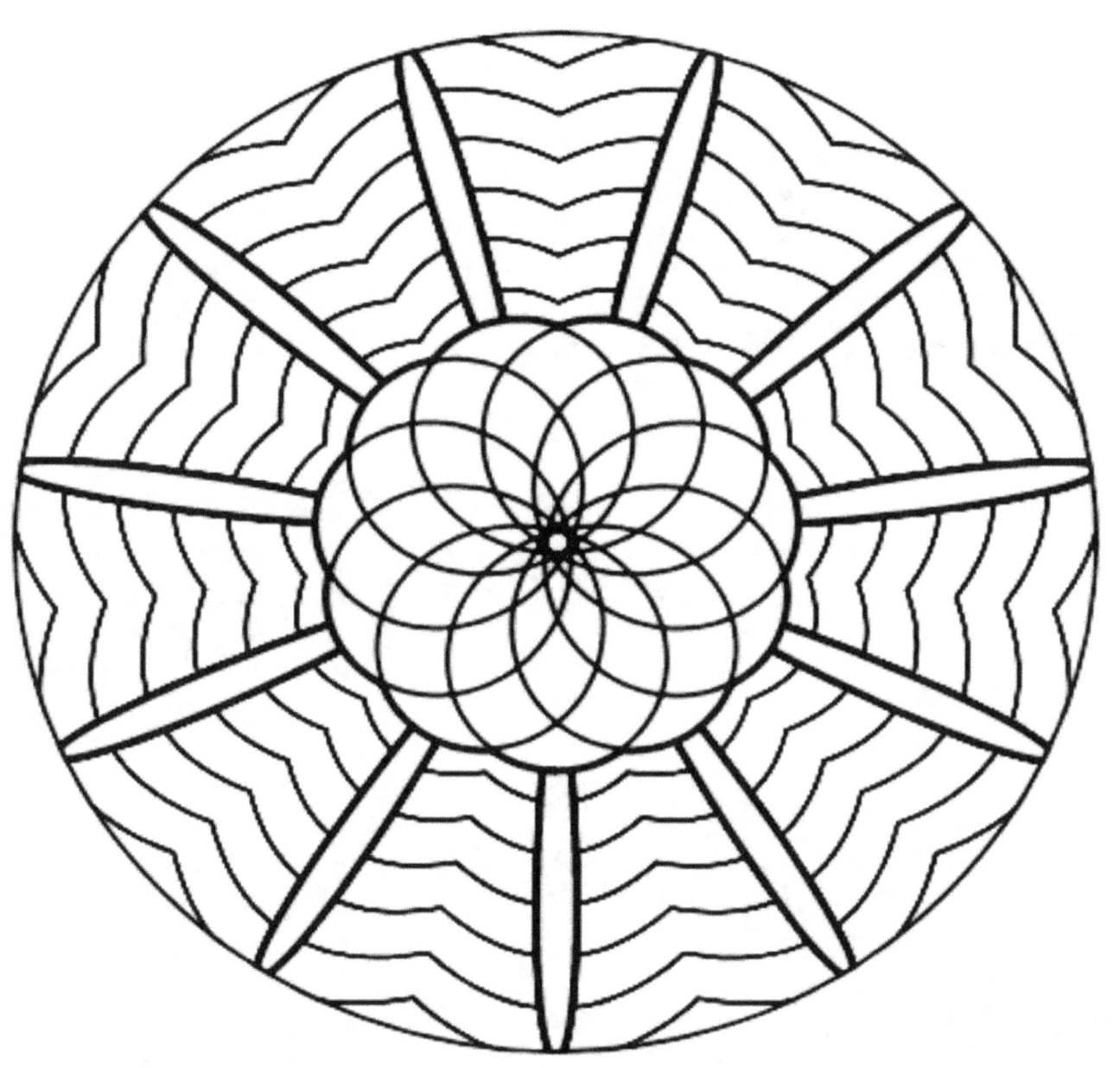

BLANK

PAGE

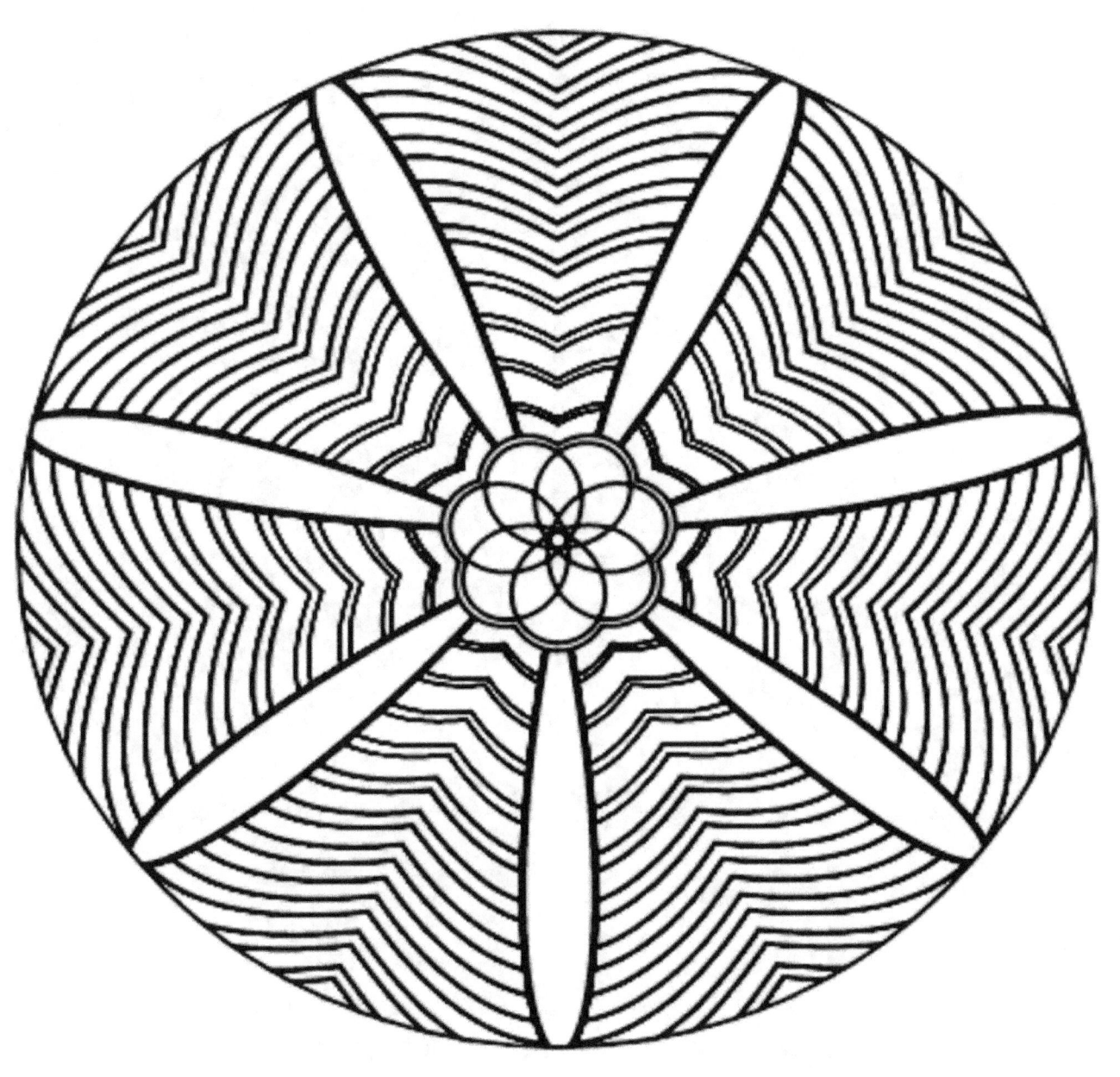

BLANK

PAGE

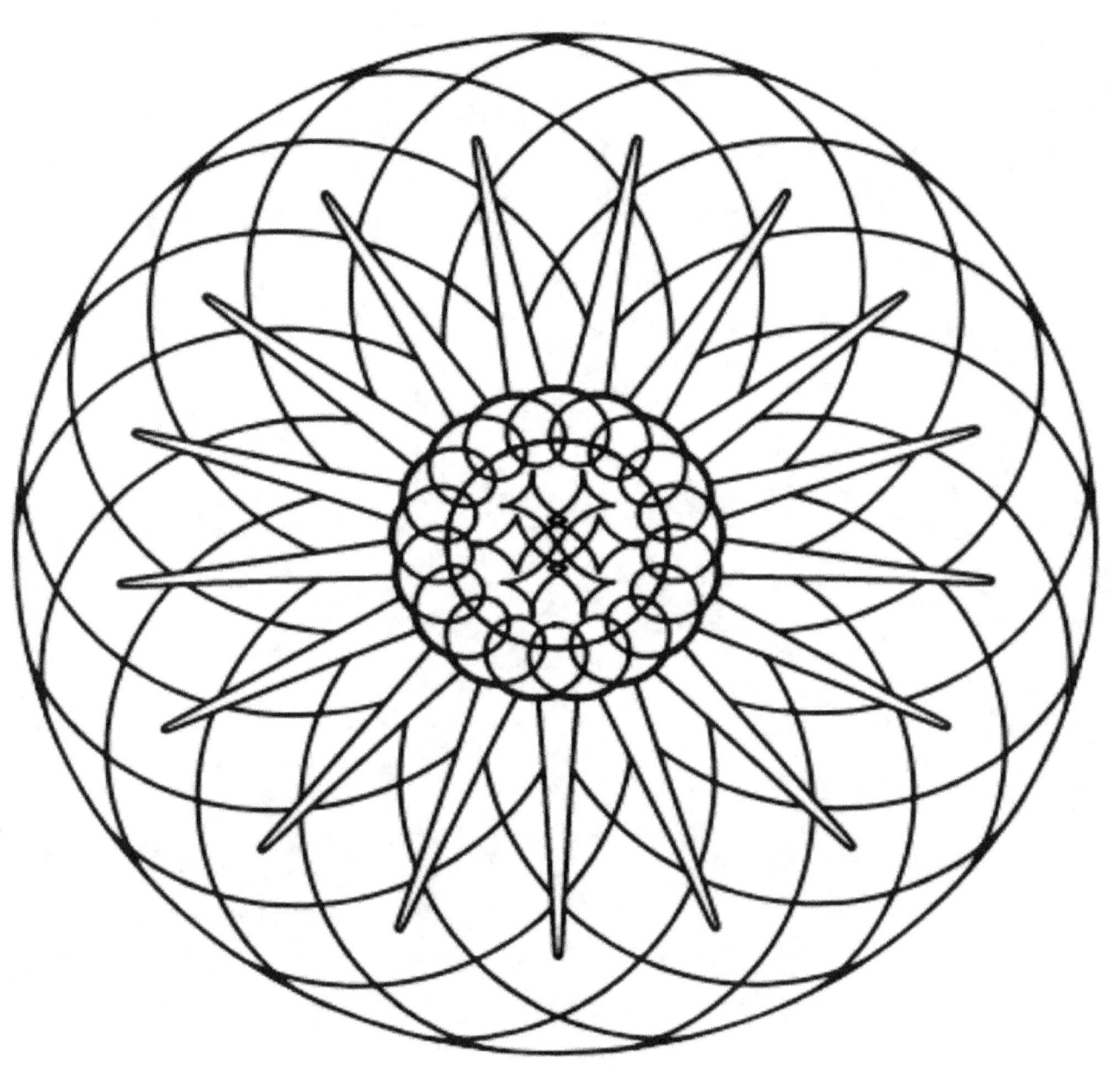

BLANK

PAGE

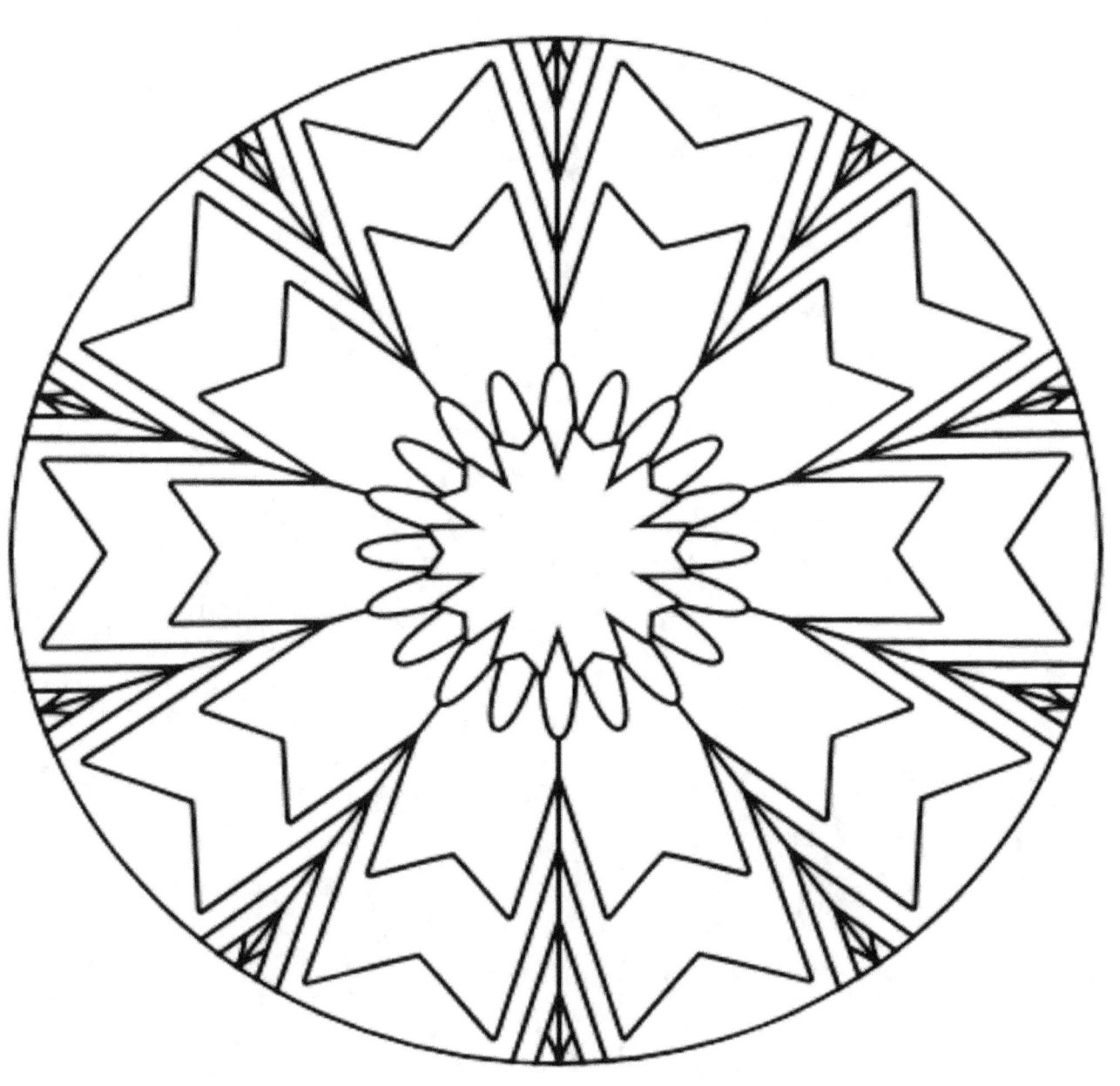

BLANK

PAGE

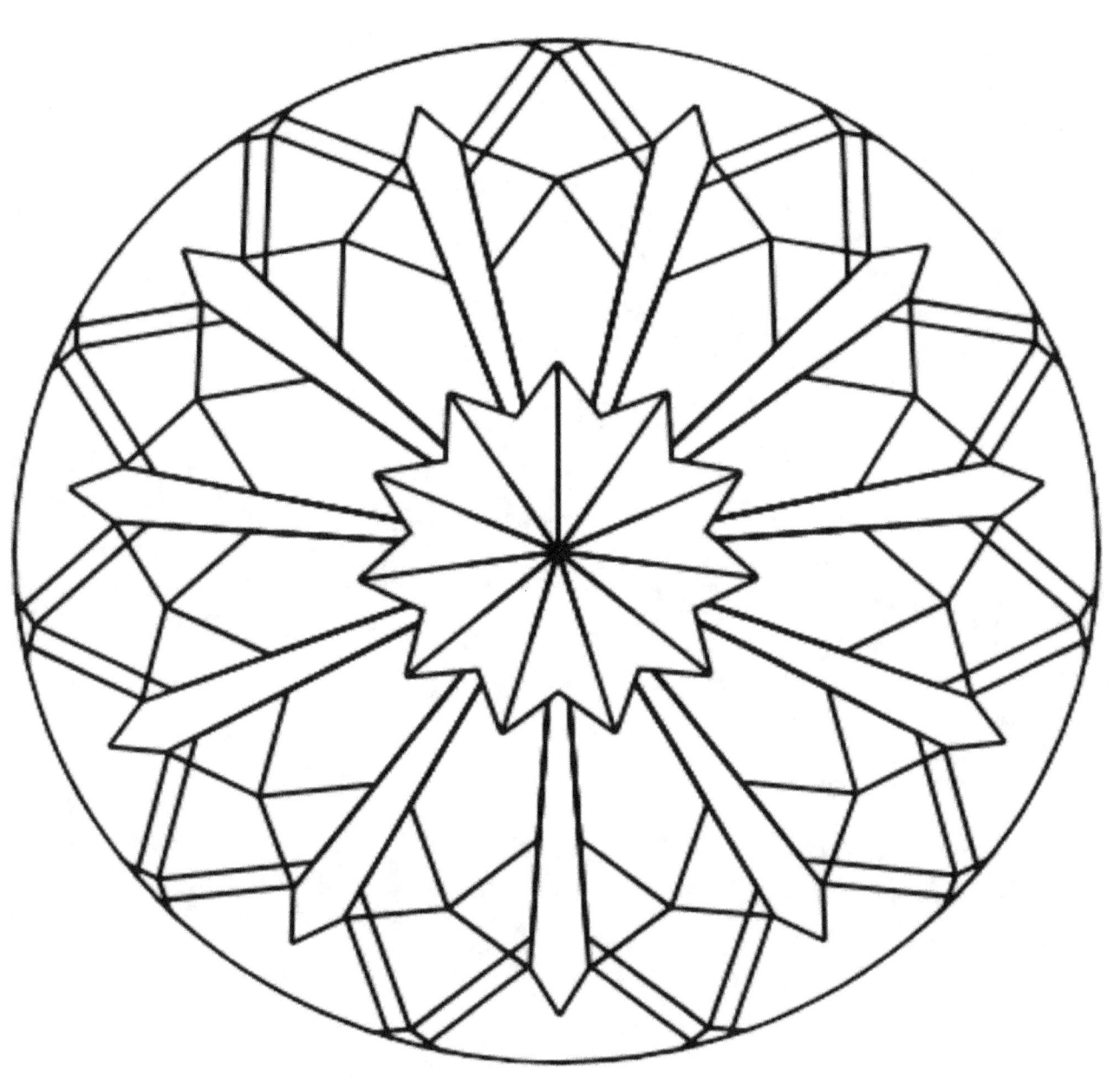

BLANK PAGE

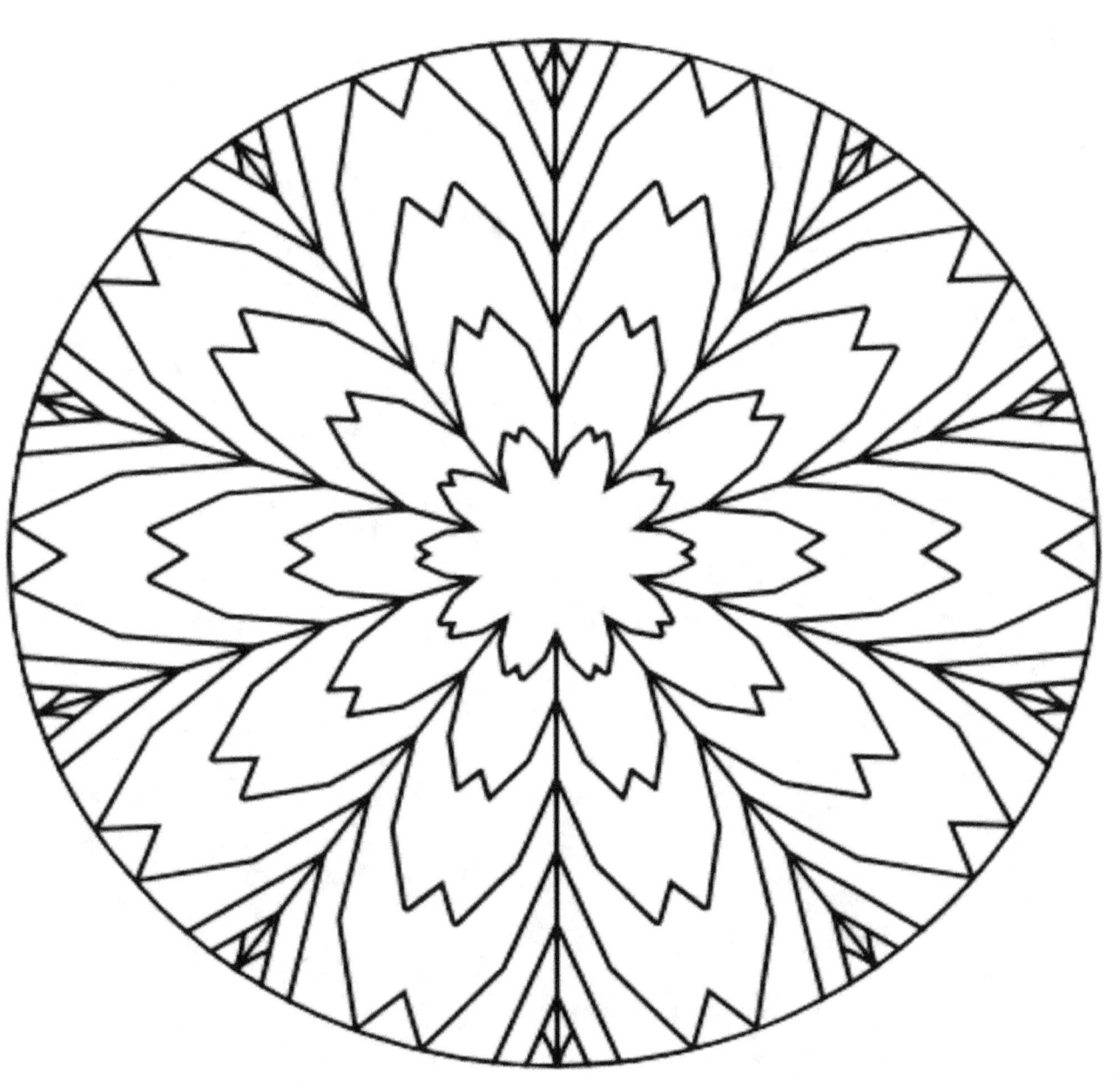

BLANK PAGE

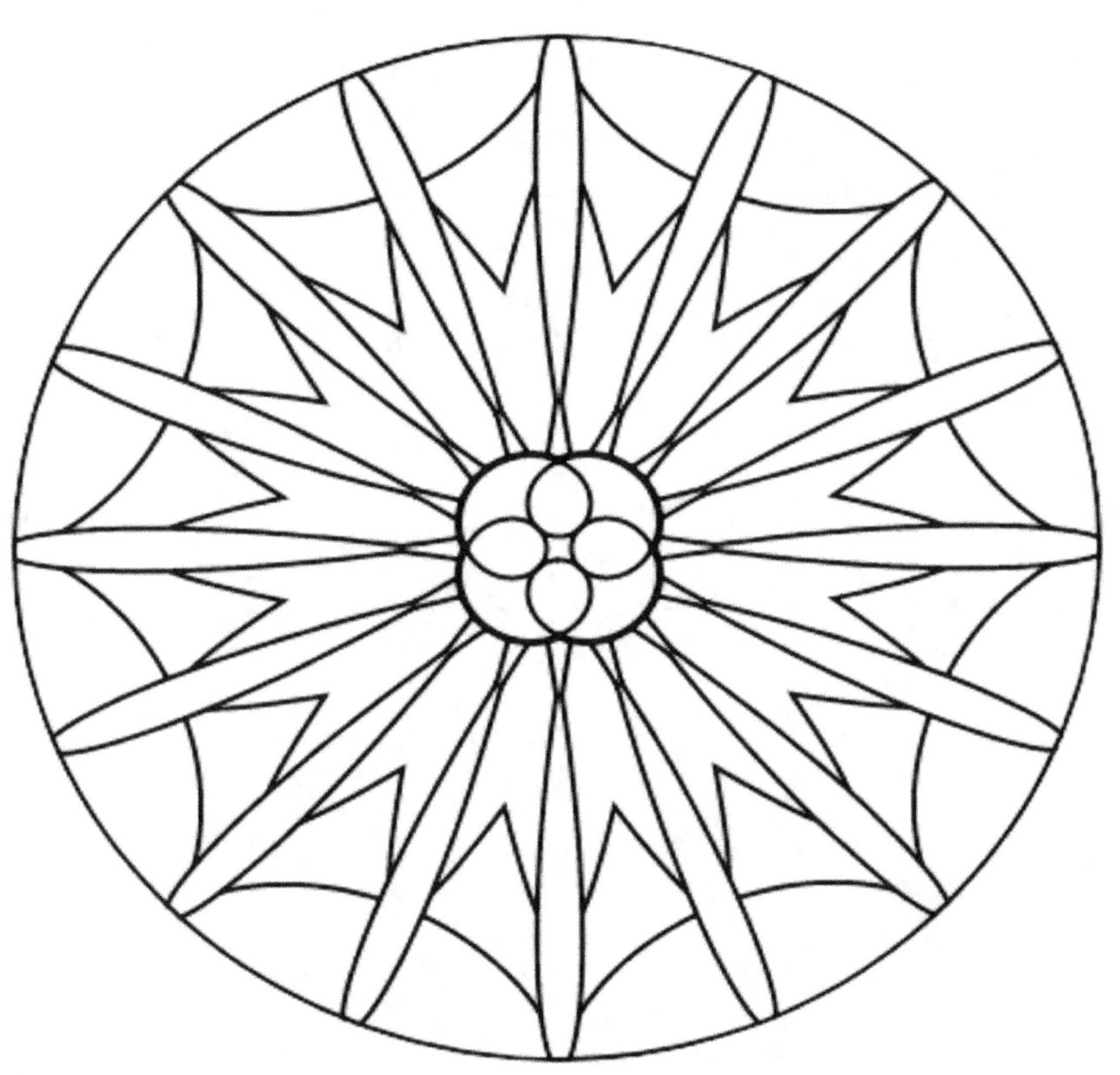

BLANK

PAGE

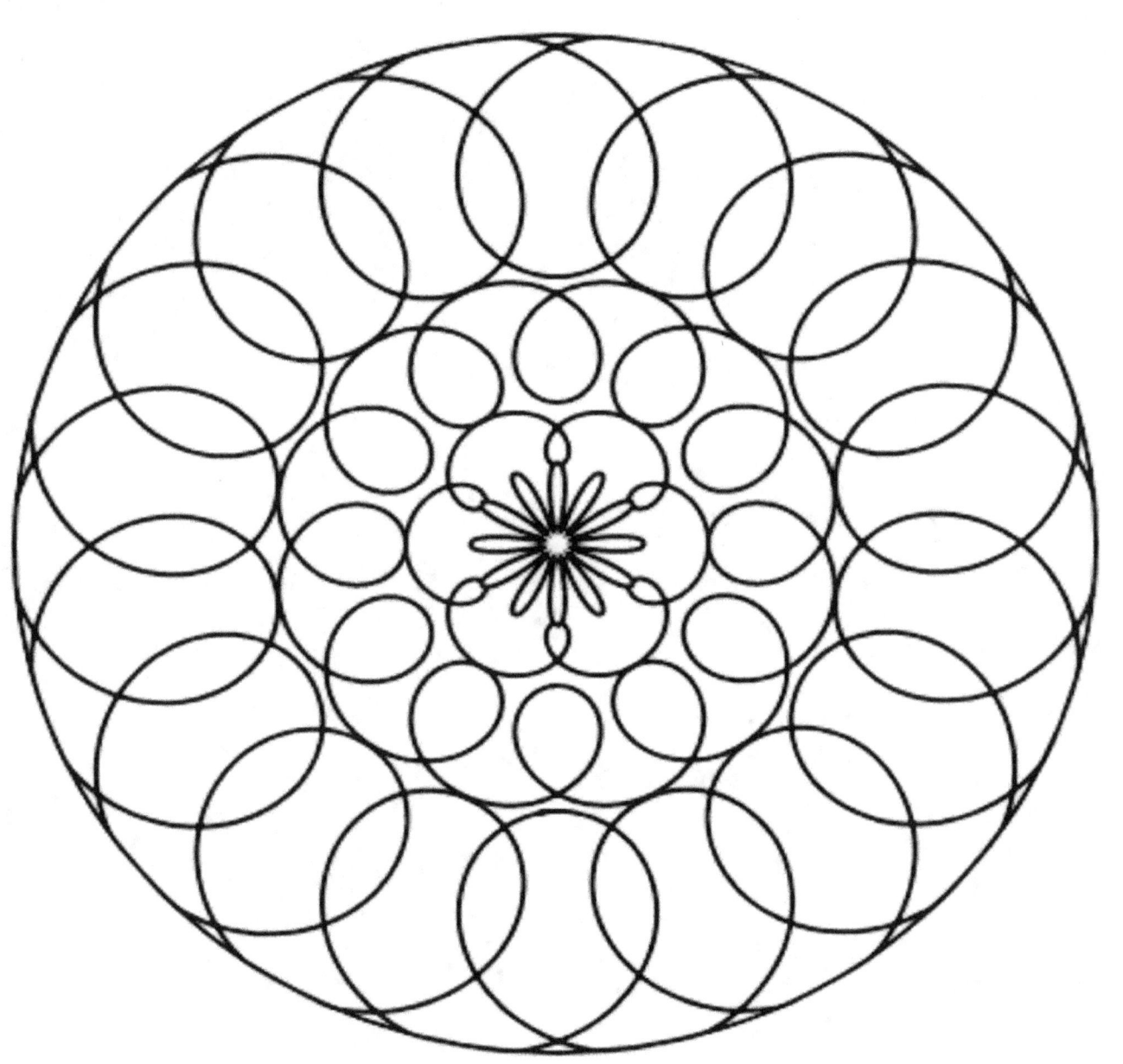

BLANK

PAGE

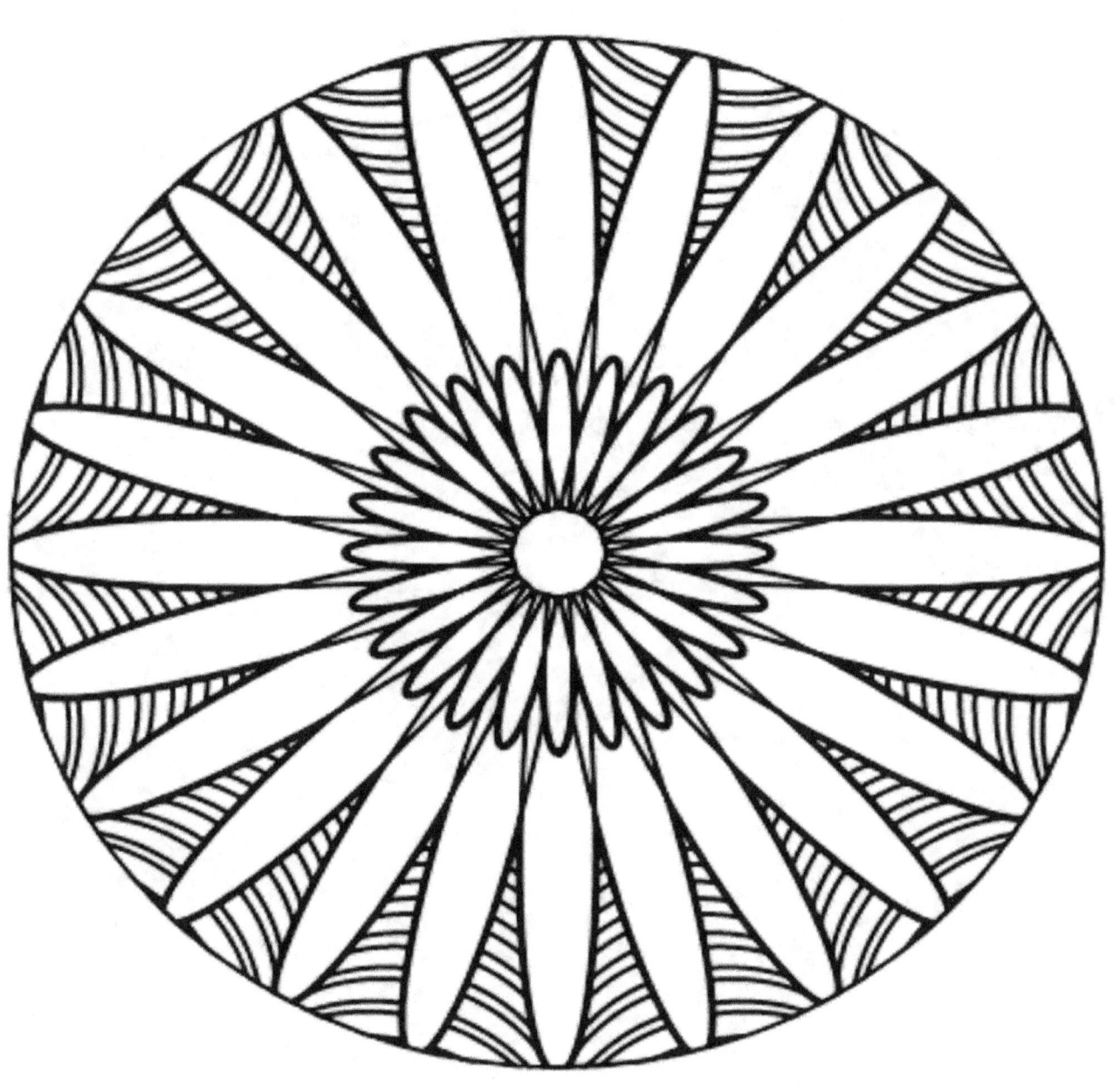

BLANK

PAGE

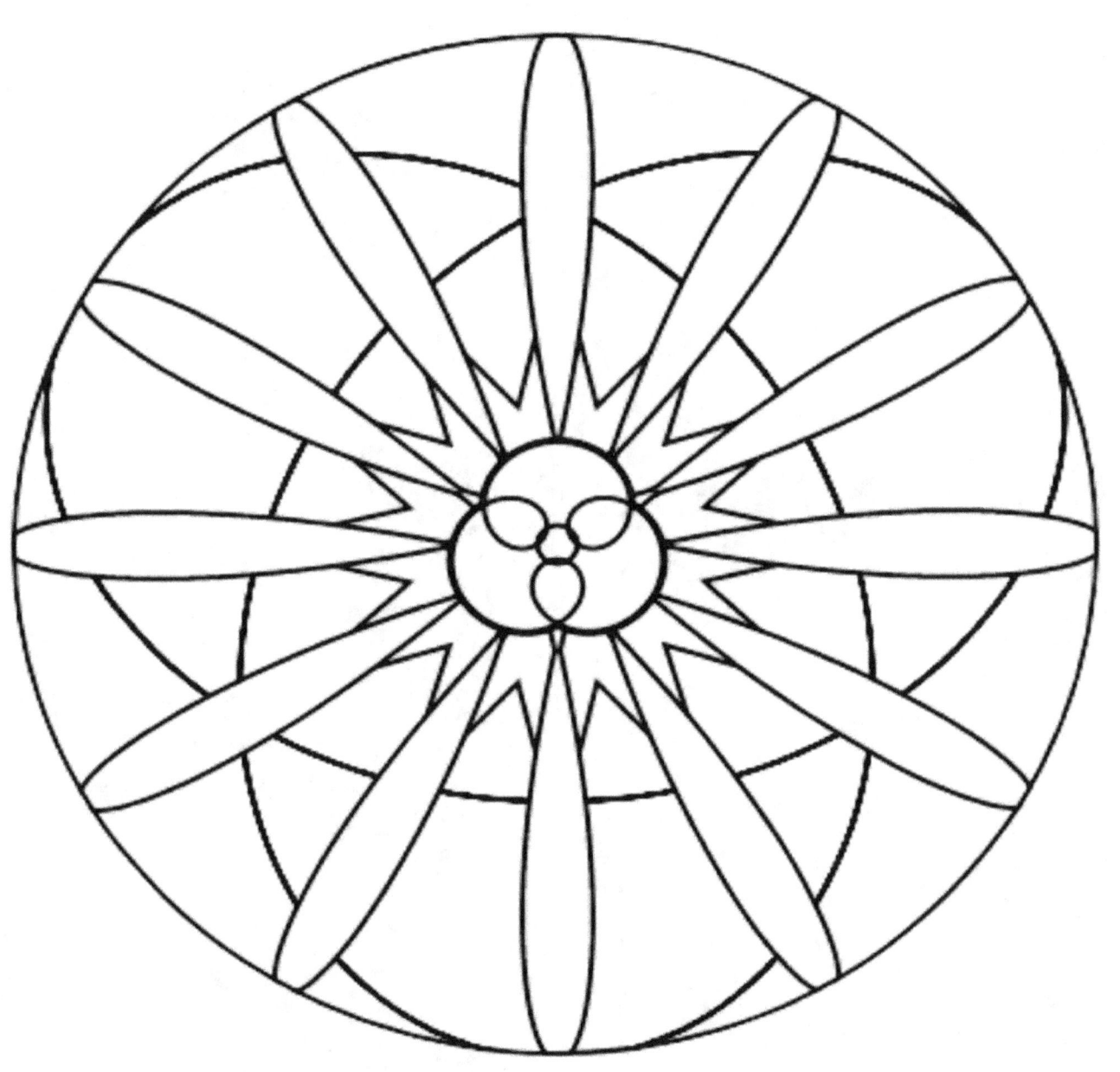

BLANK

PAGE

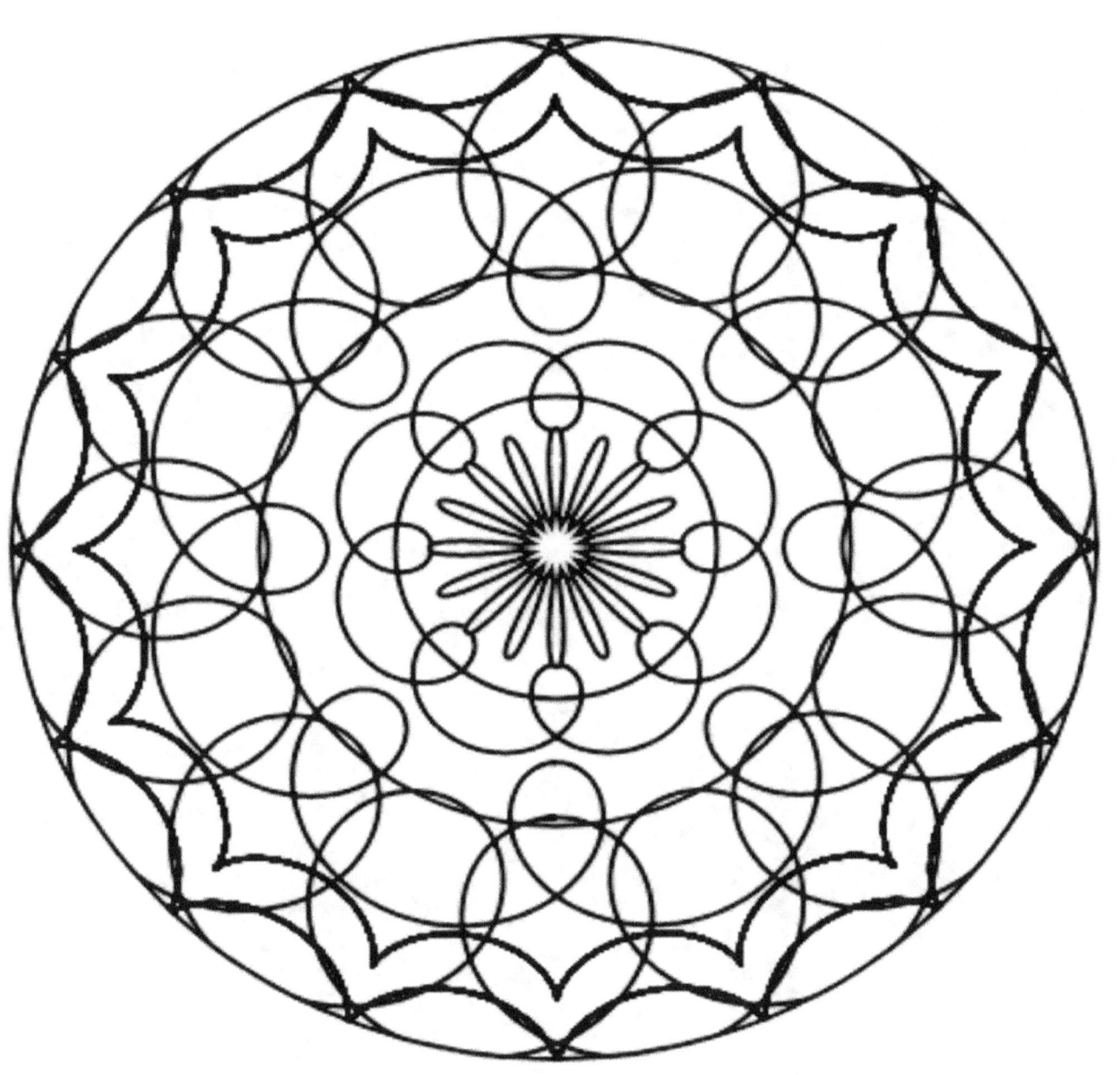

BLANK

PAGE

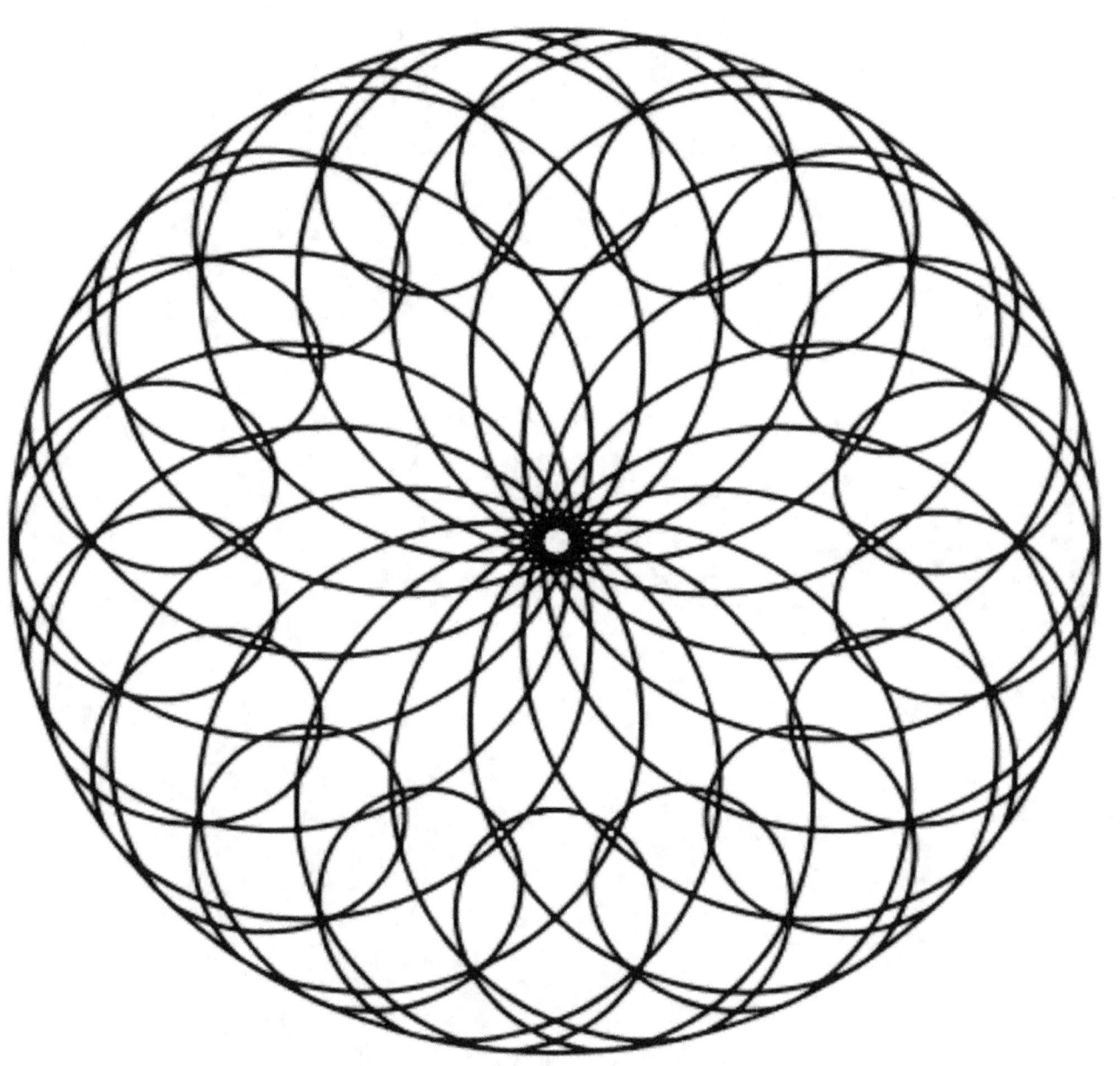

BLANK

PAGE

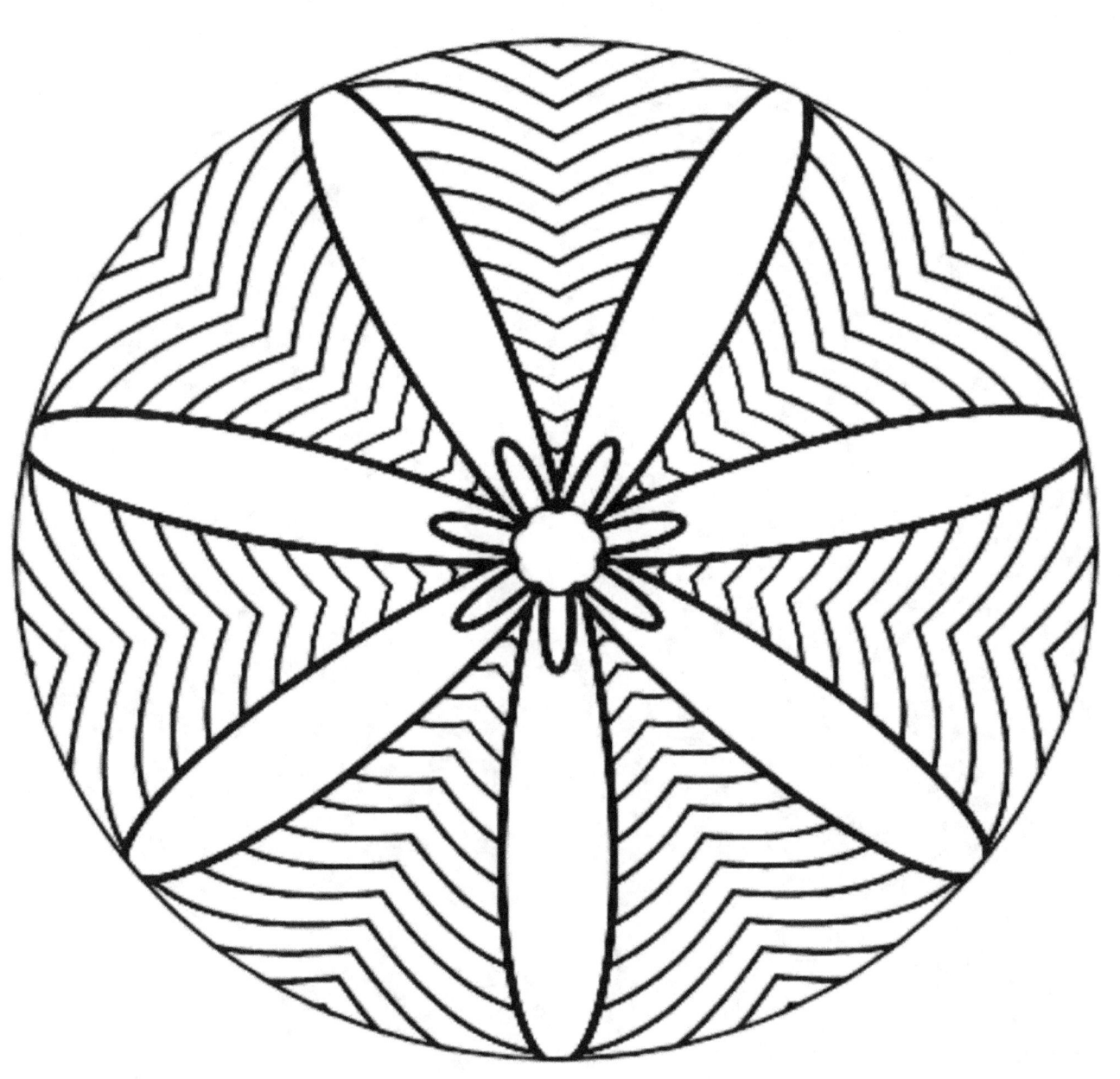

BLANK

PAGE

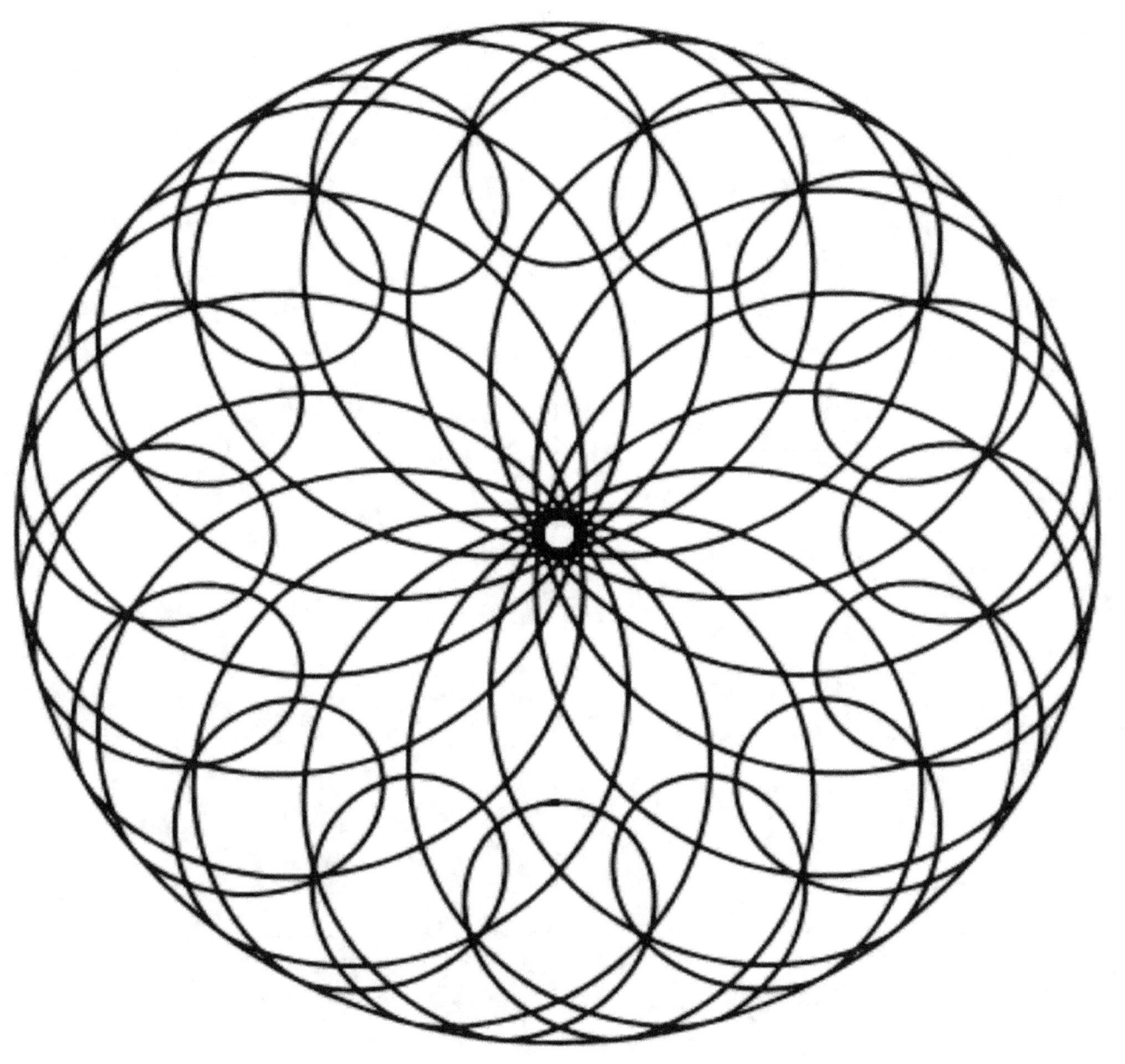

BLANK

PAGE

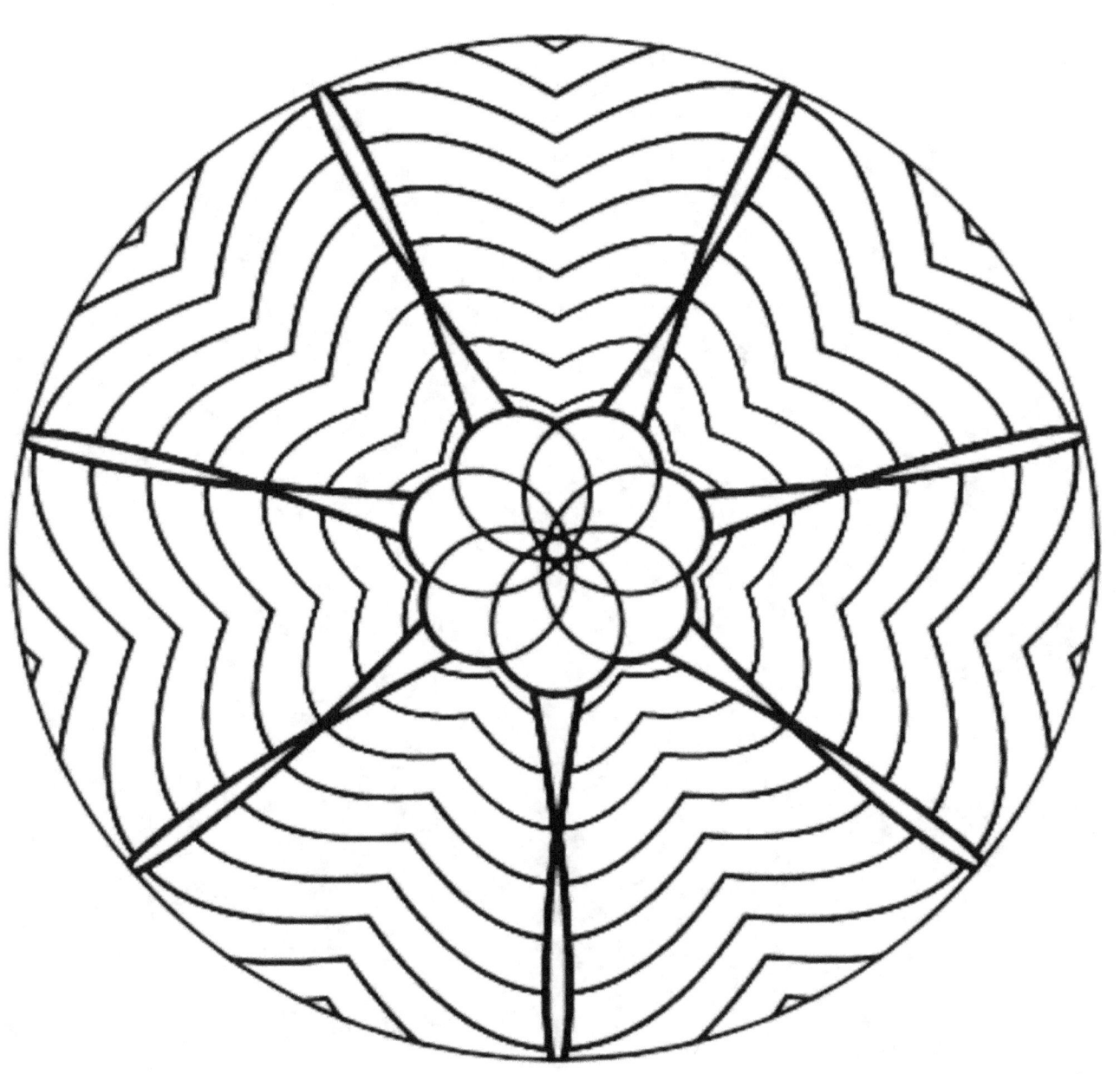

BLANK

PAGE

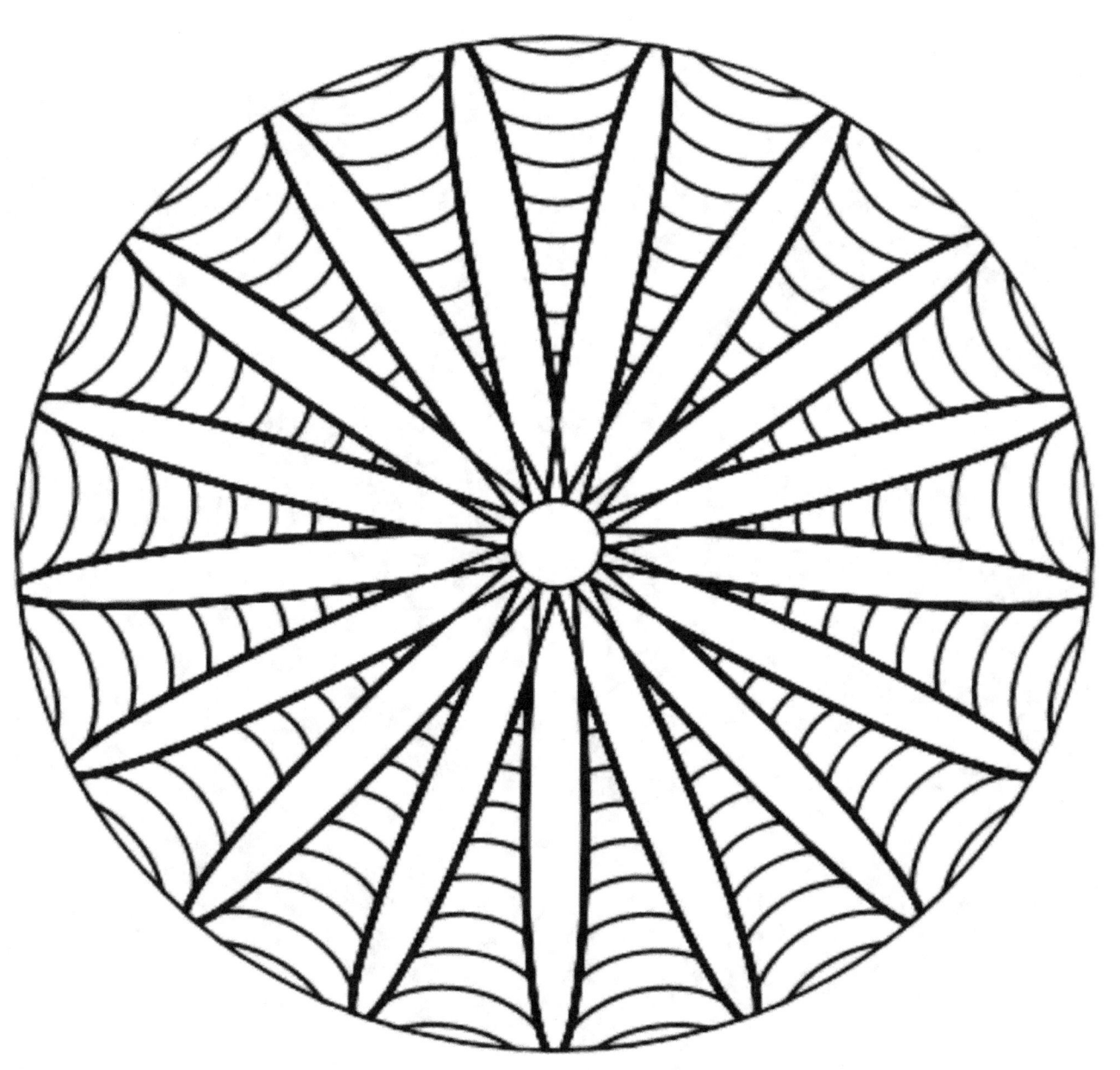

BLANK

PAGE

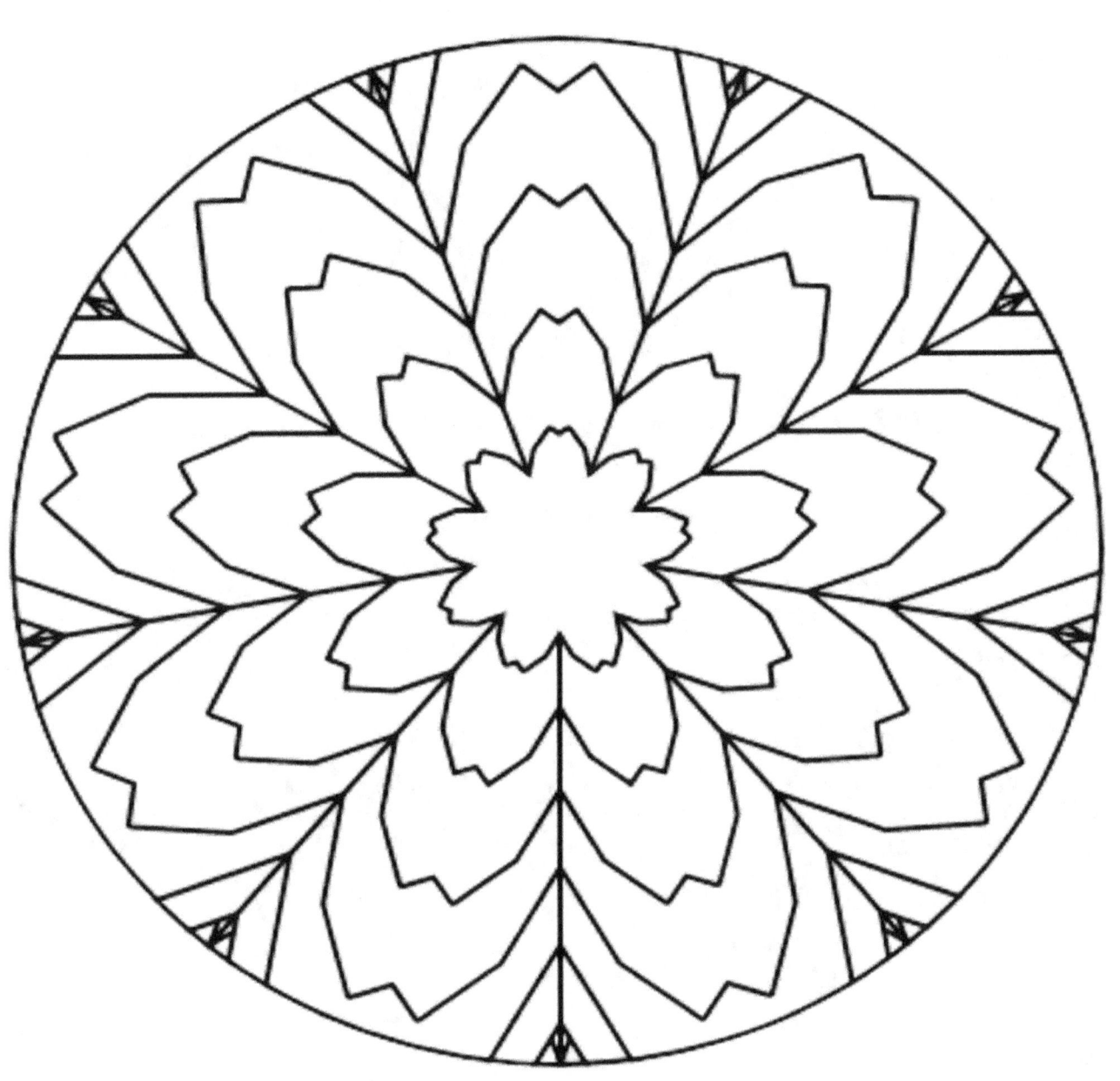

BLANK

PAGE

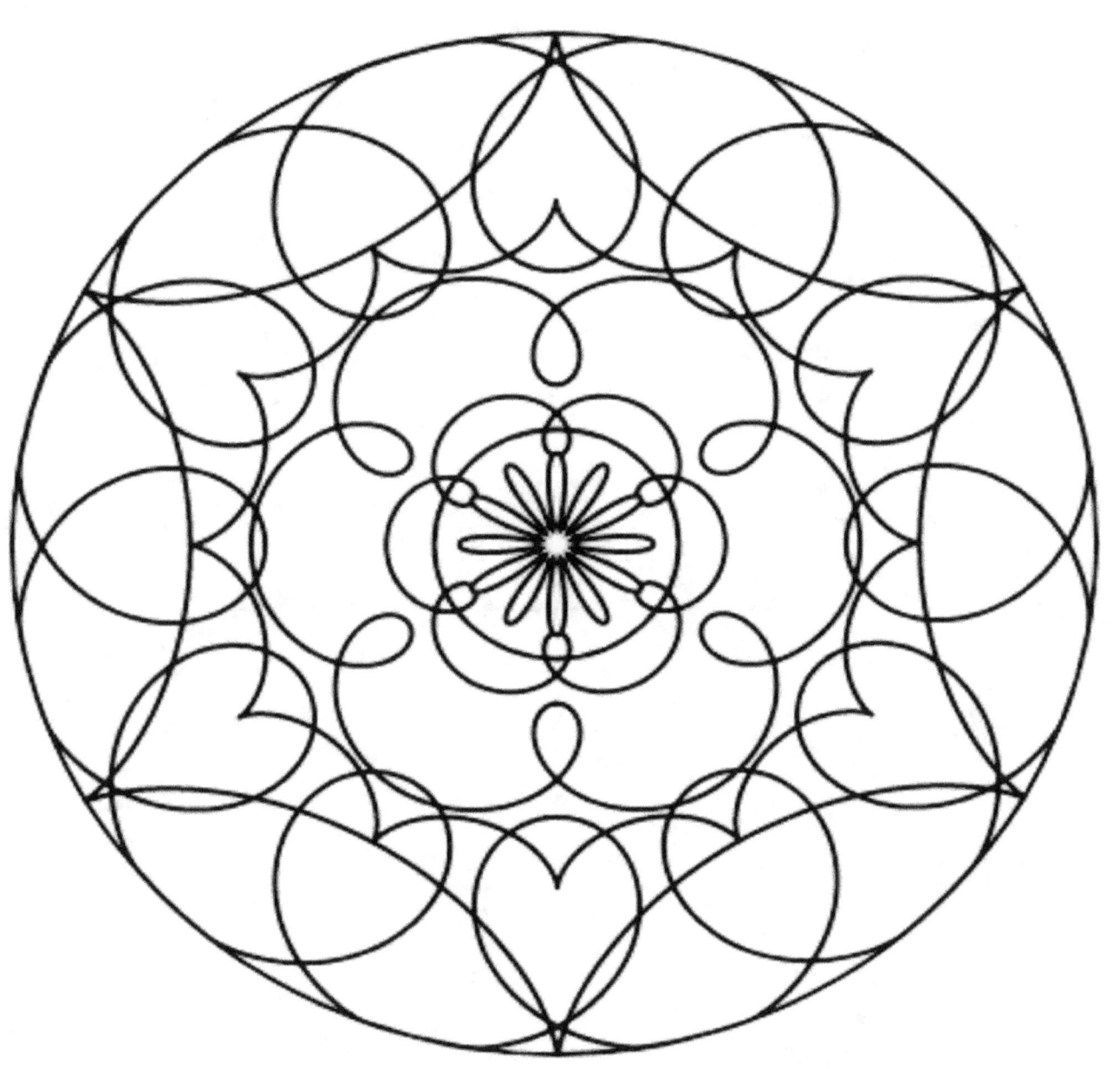

BLANK

PAGE

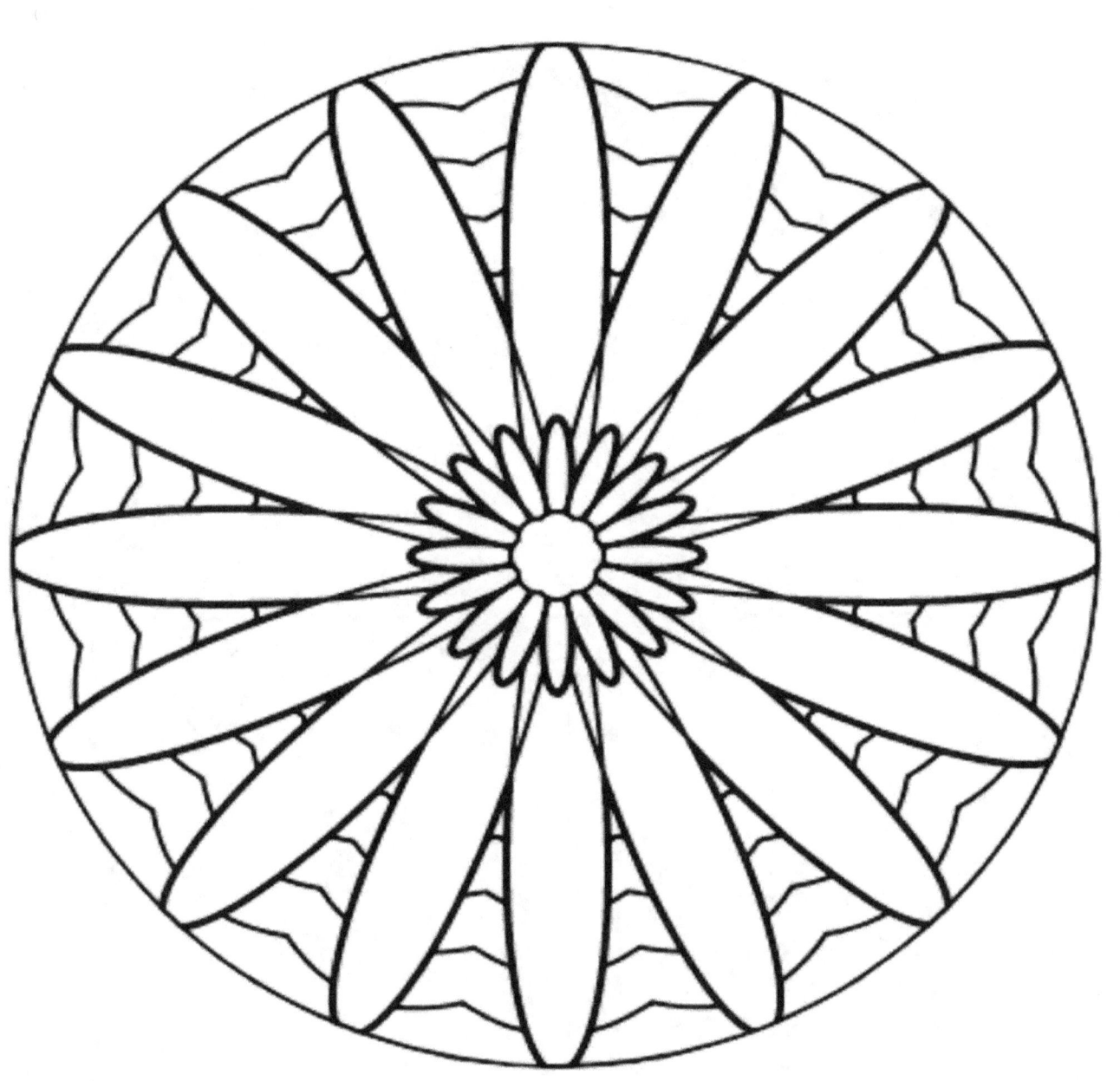

BLANK

PAGE

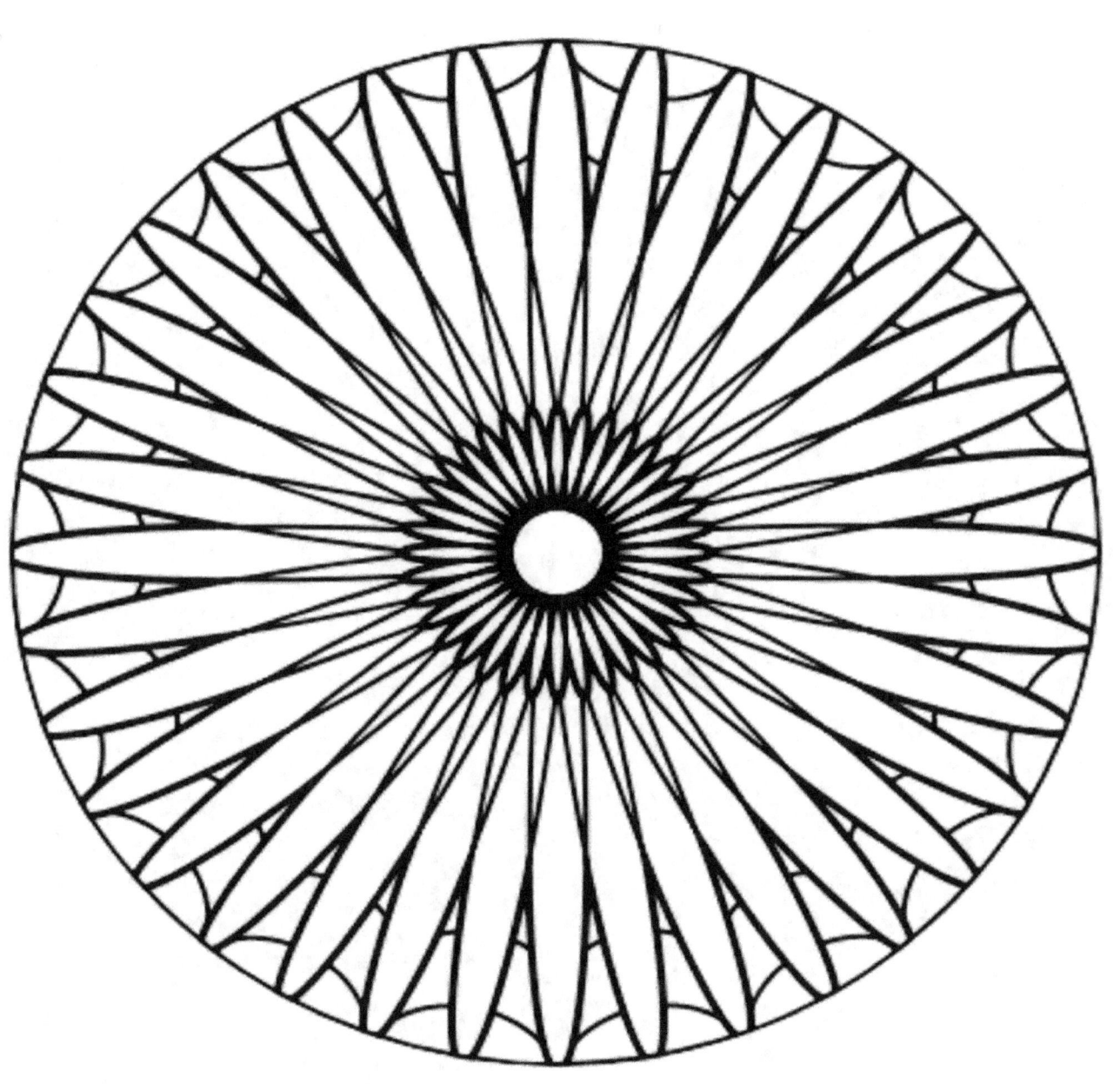

BLANK

PAGE

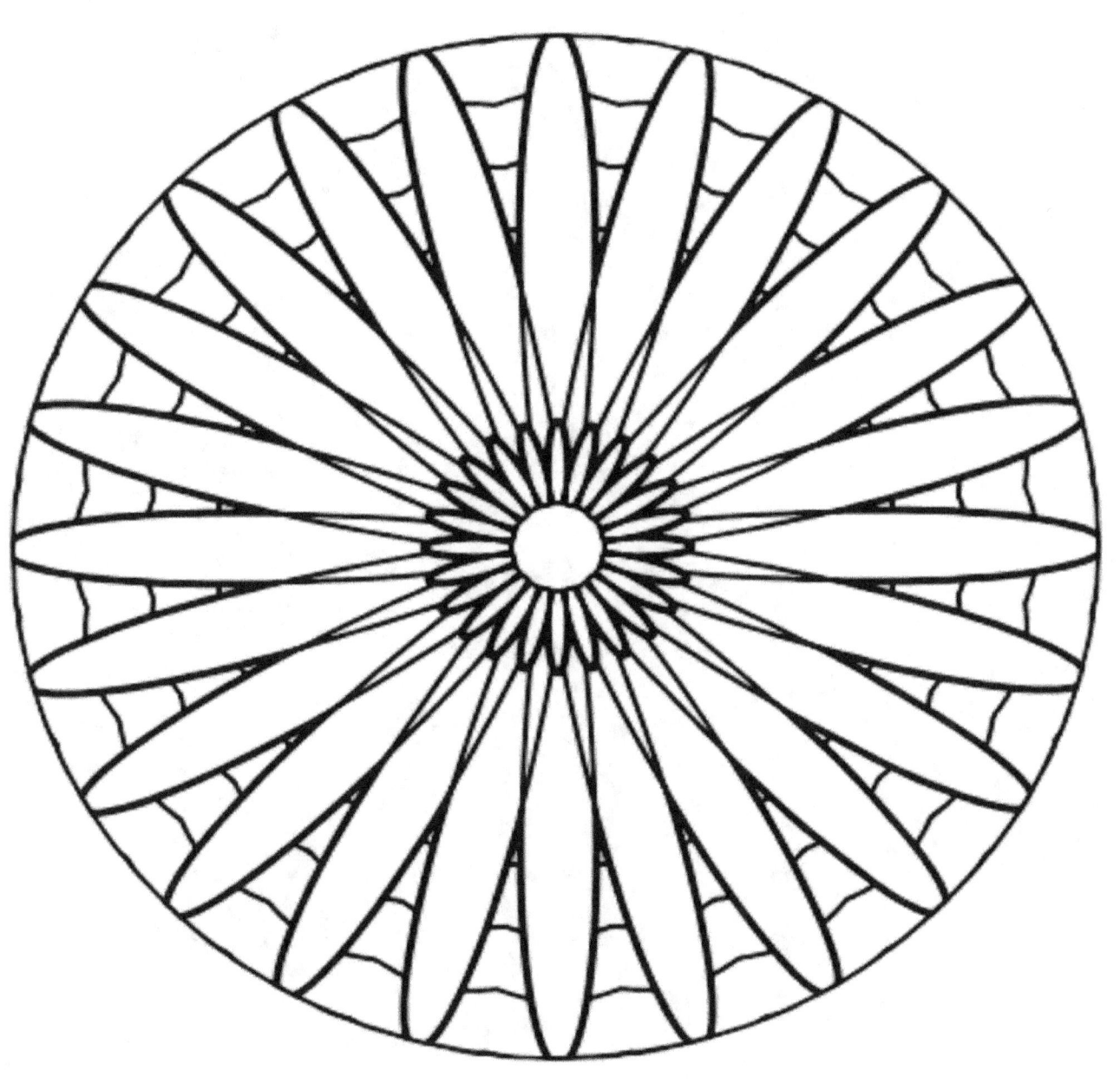

BLANK

PAGE

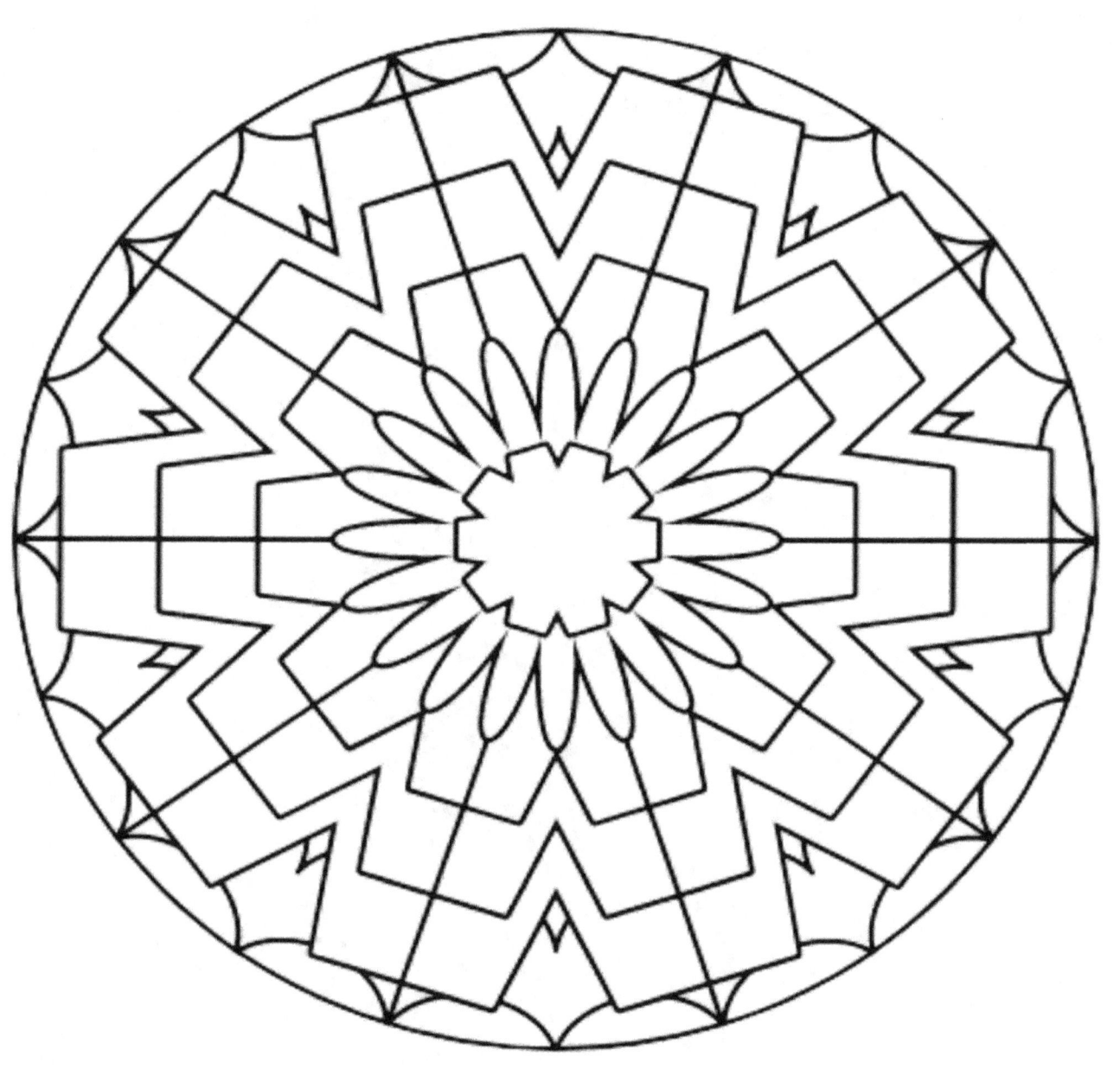

BLANK

PAGE

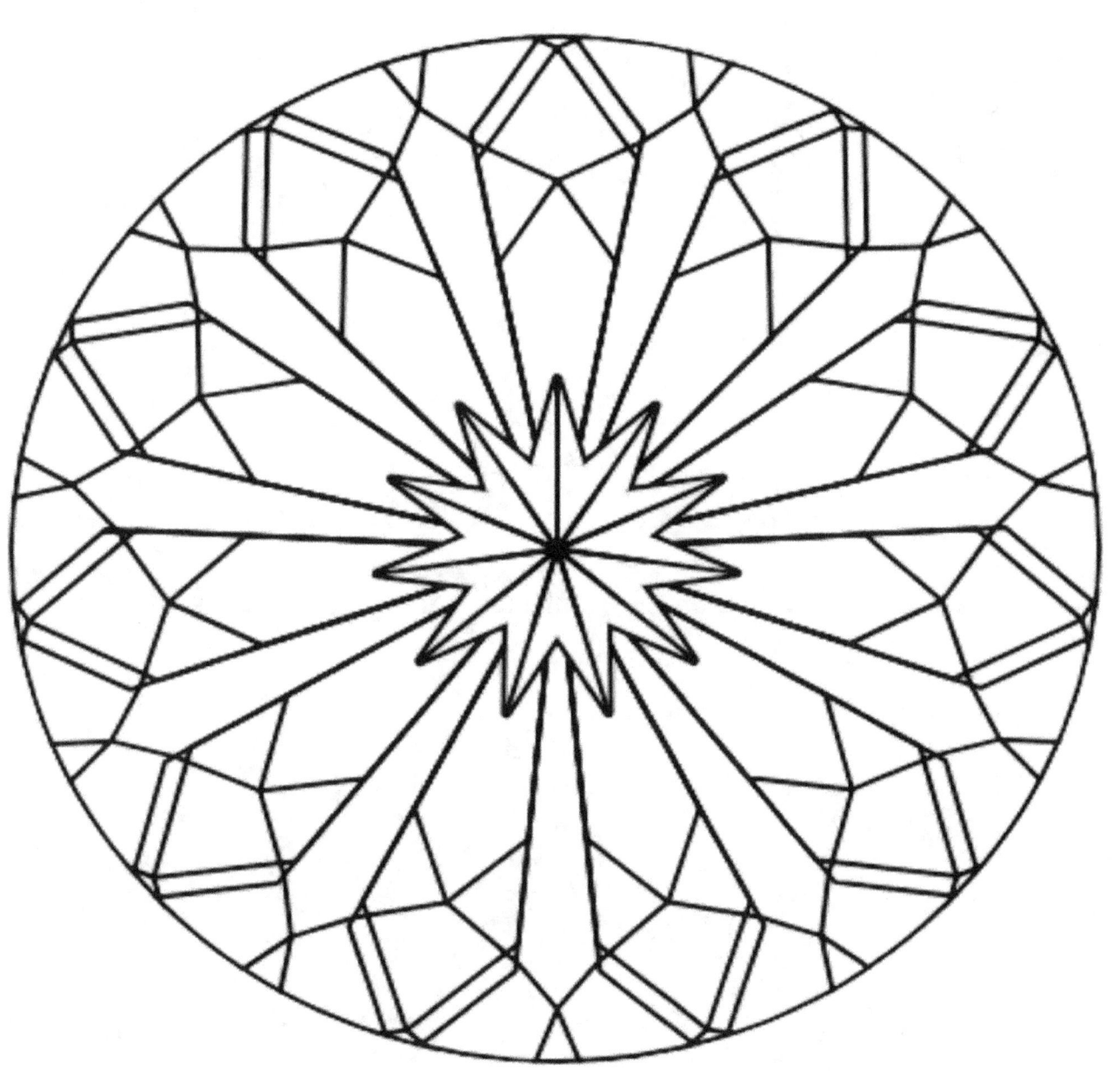

BLANK

PAGE

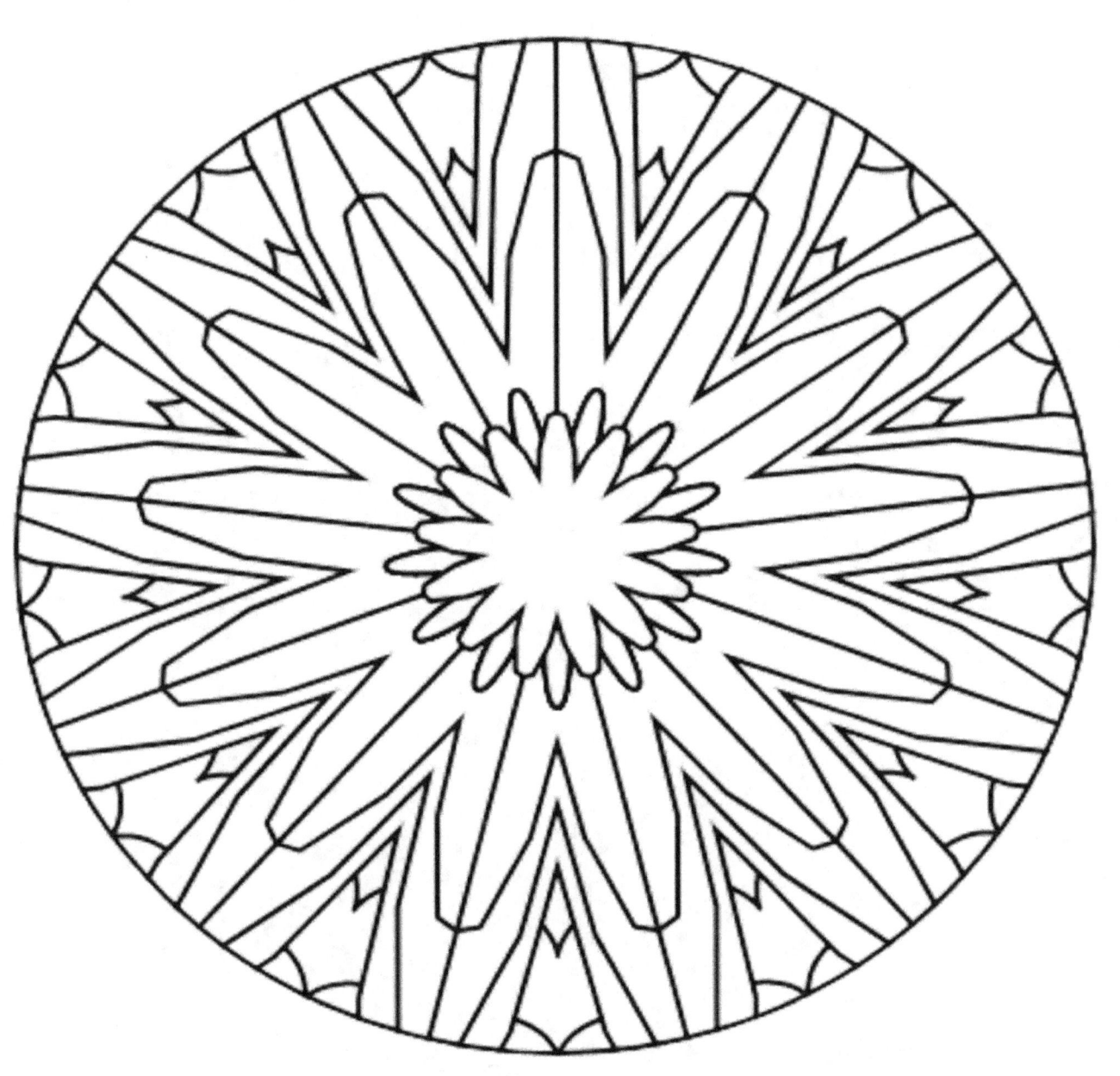

BLANK

PAGE

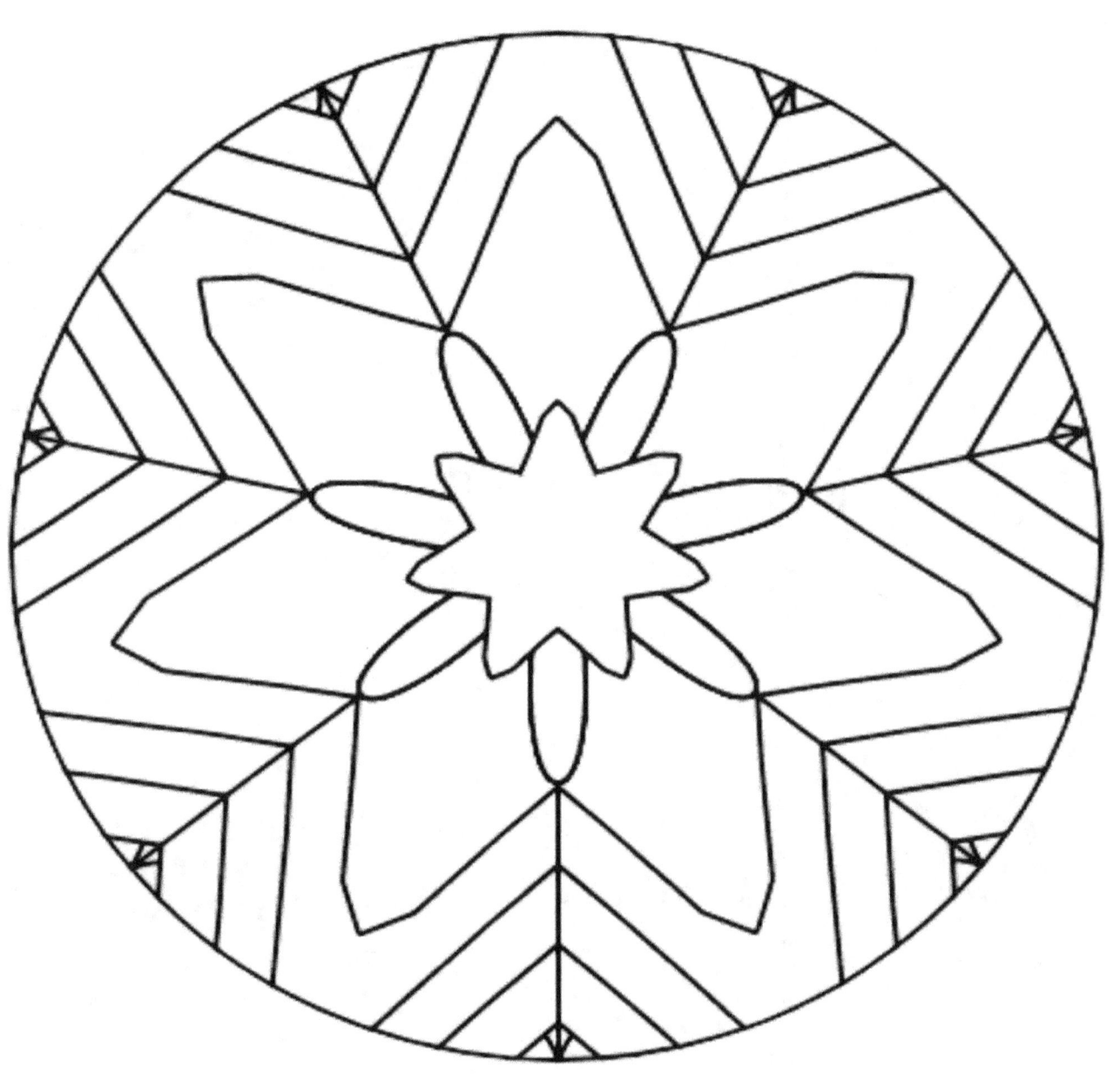

BLANK

PAGE

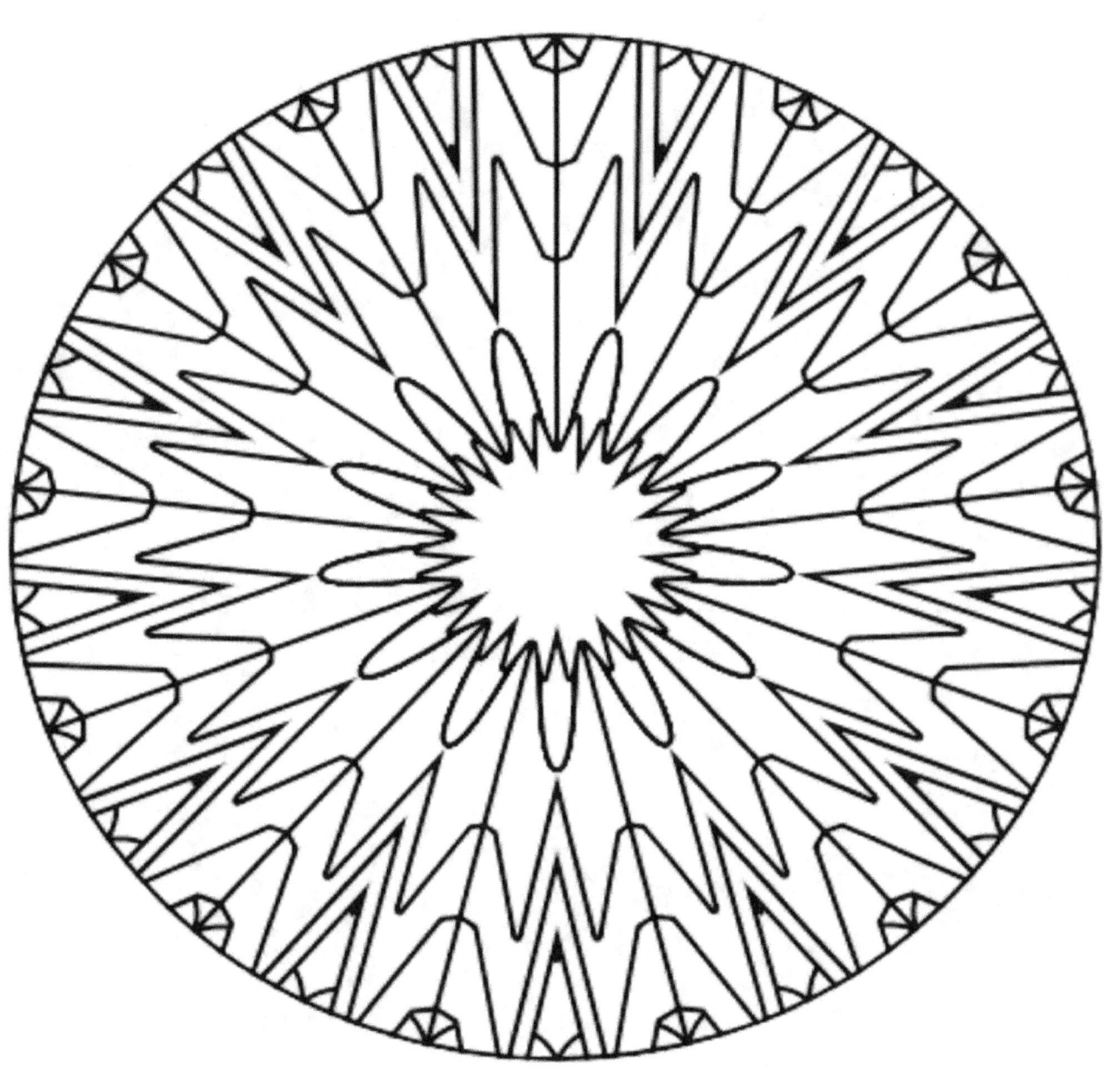

BLANK

PAGE

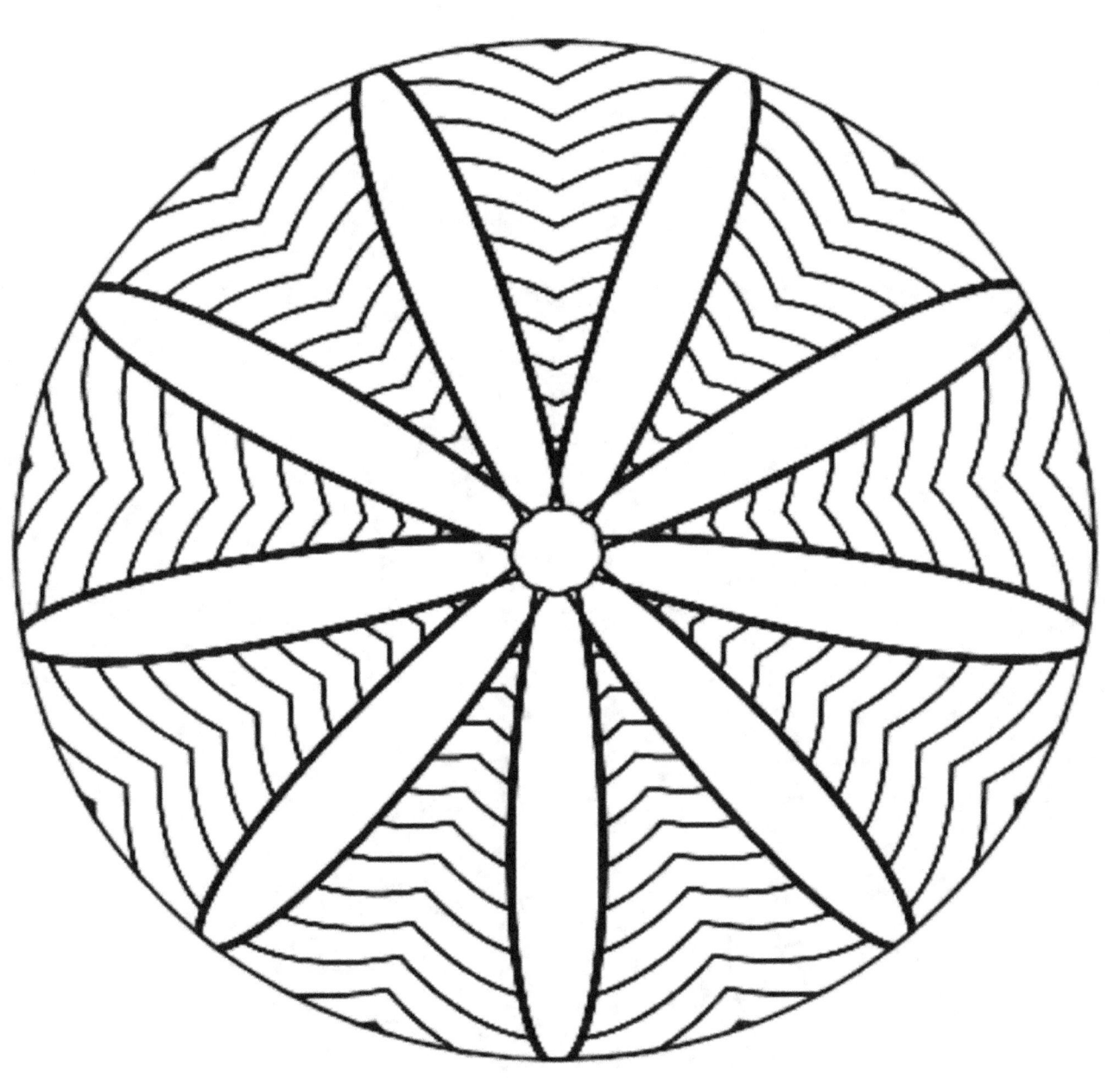

BLANK

PAGE

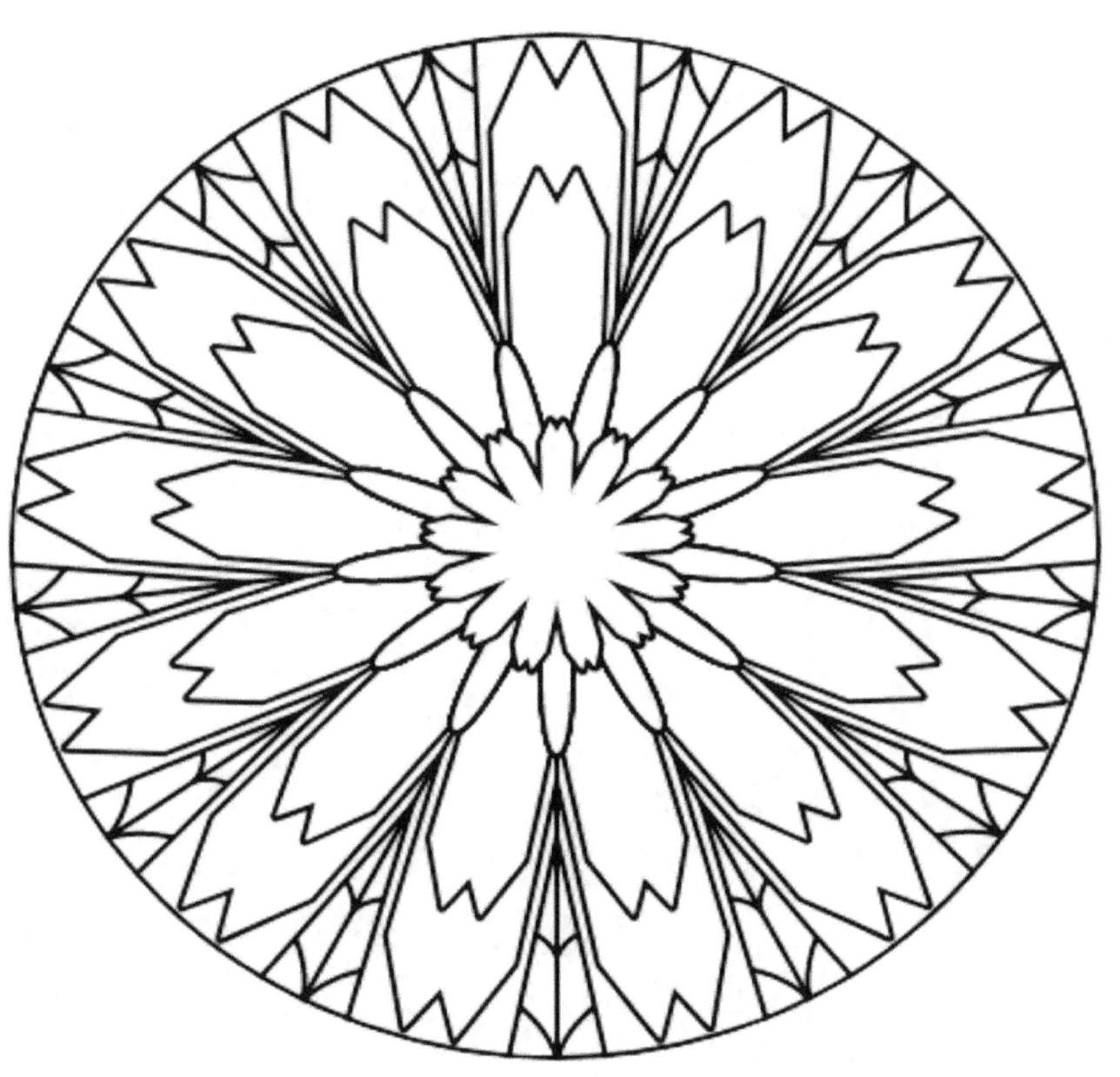

BLANK

PAGE

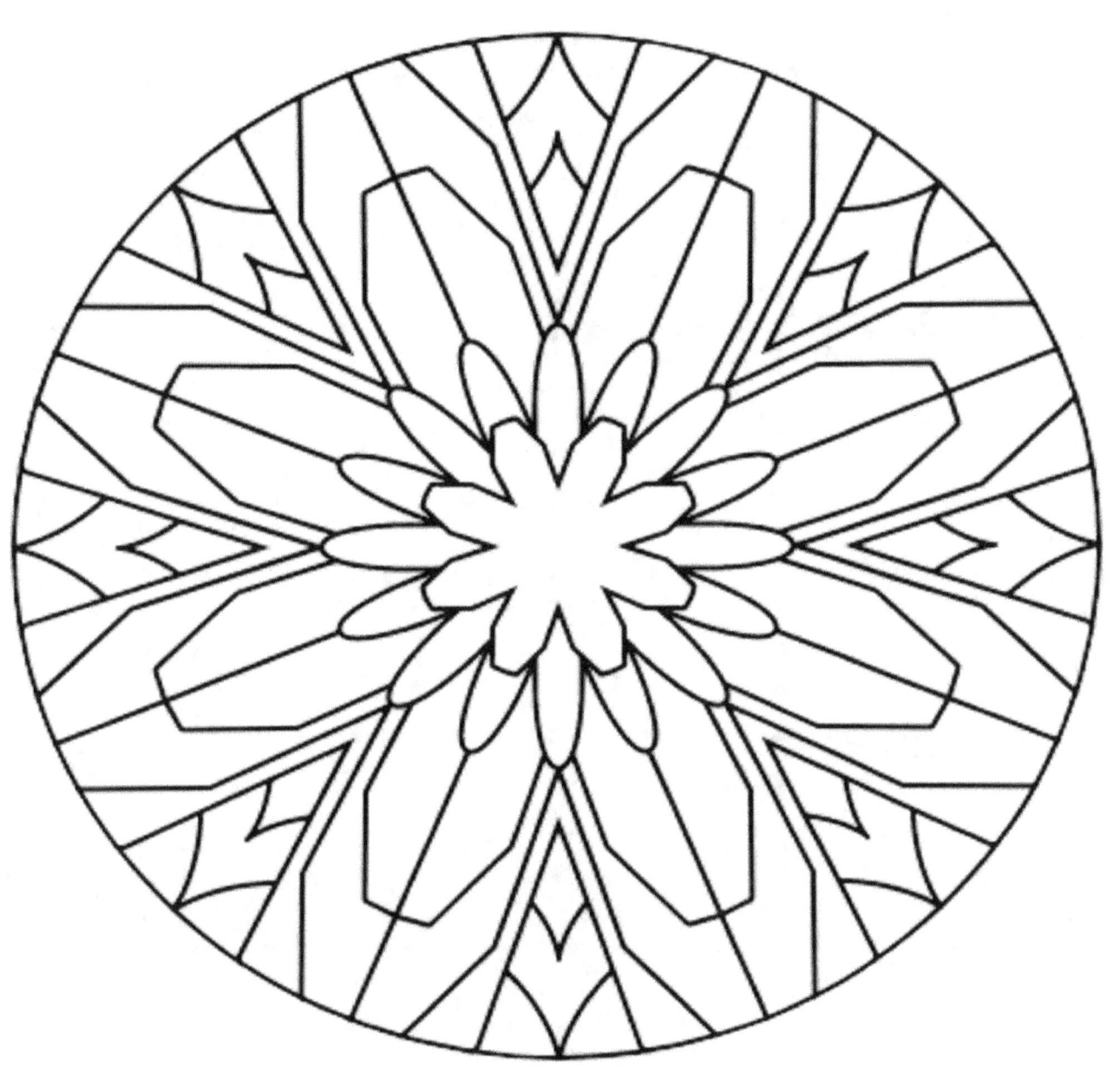

BLANK

PAGE

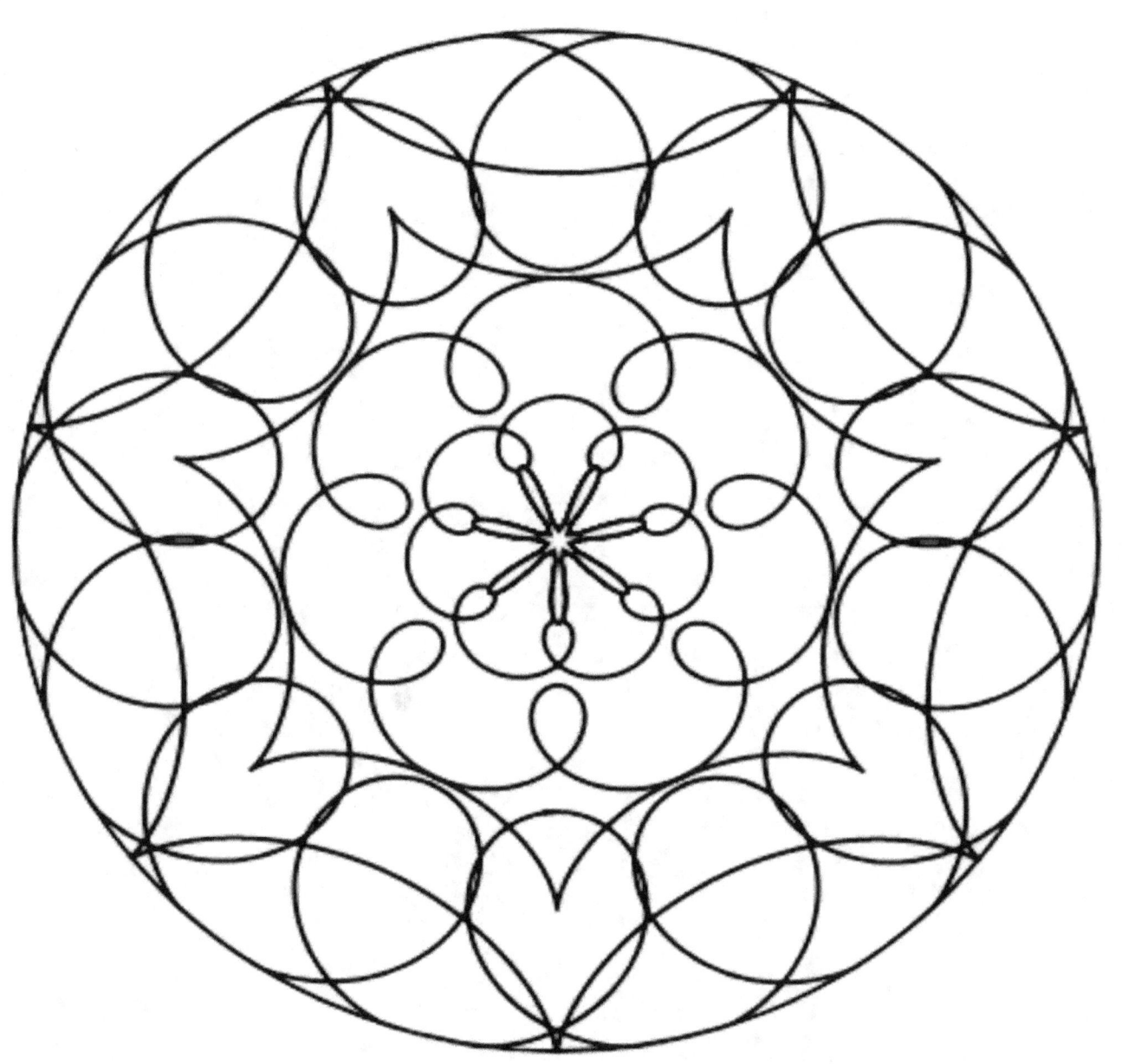

BLANK

PAGE

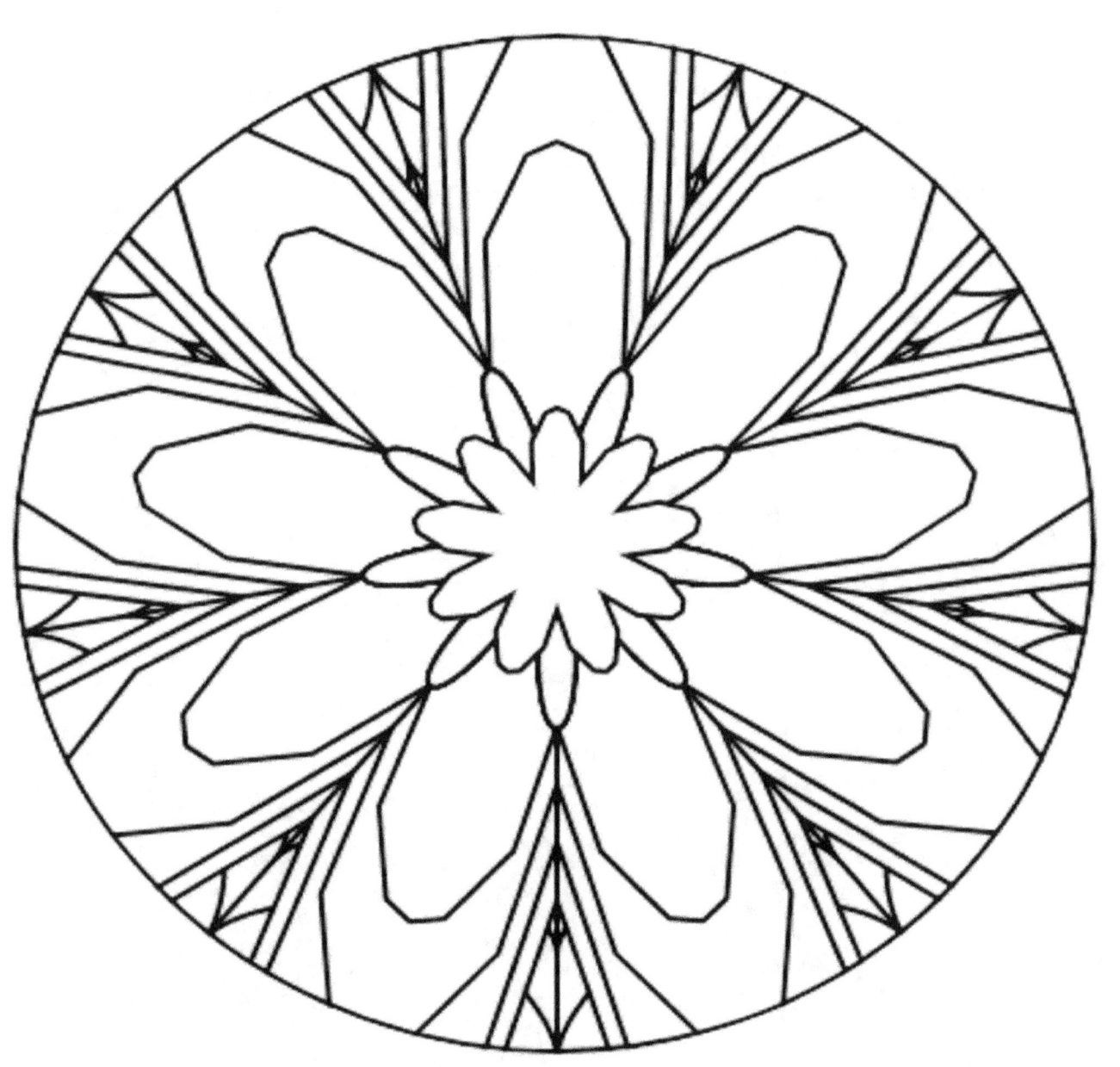

BLANK PAGE

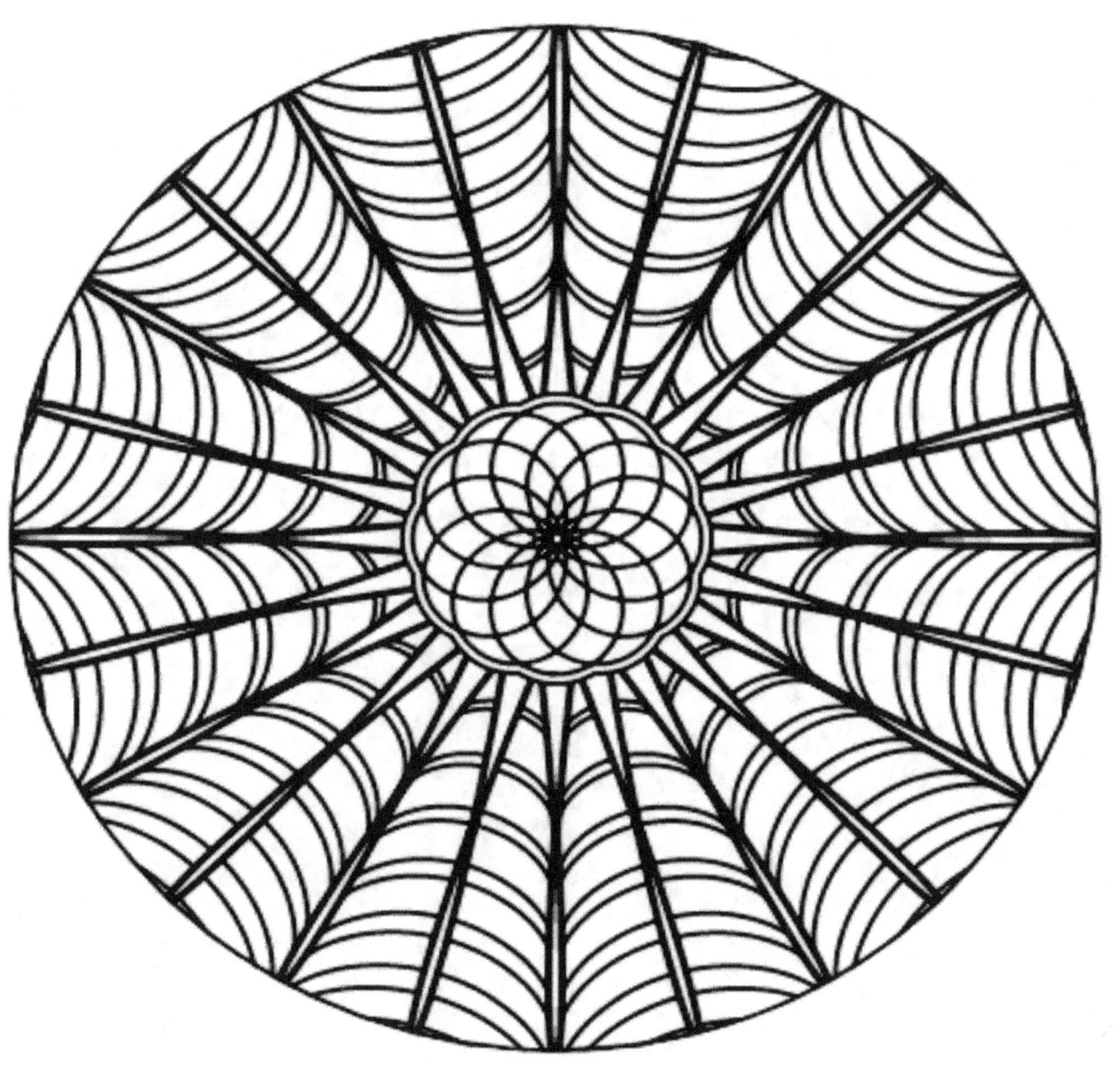

BLANK

PAGE

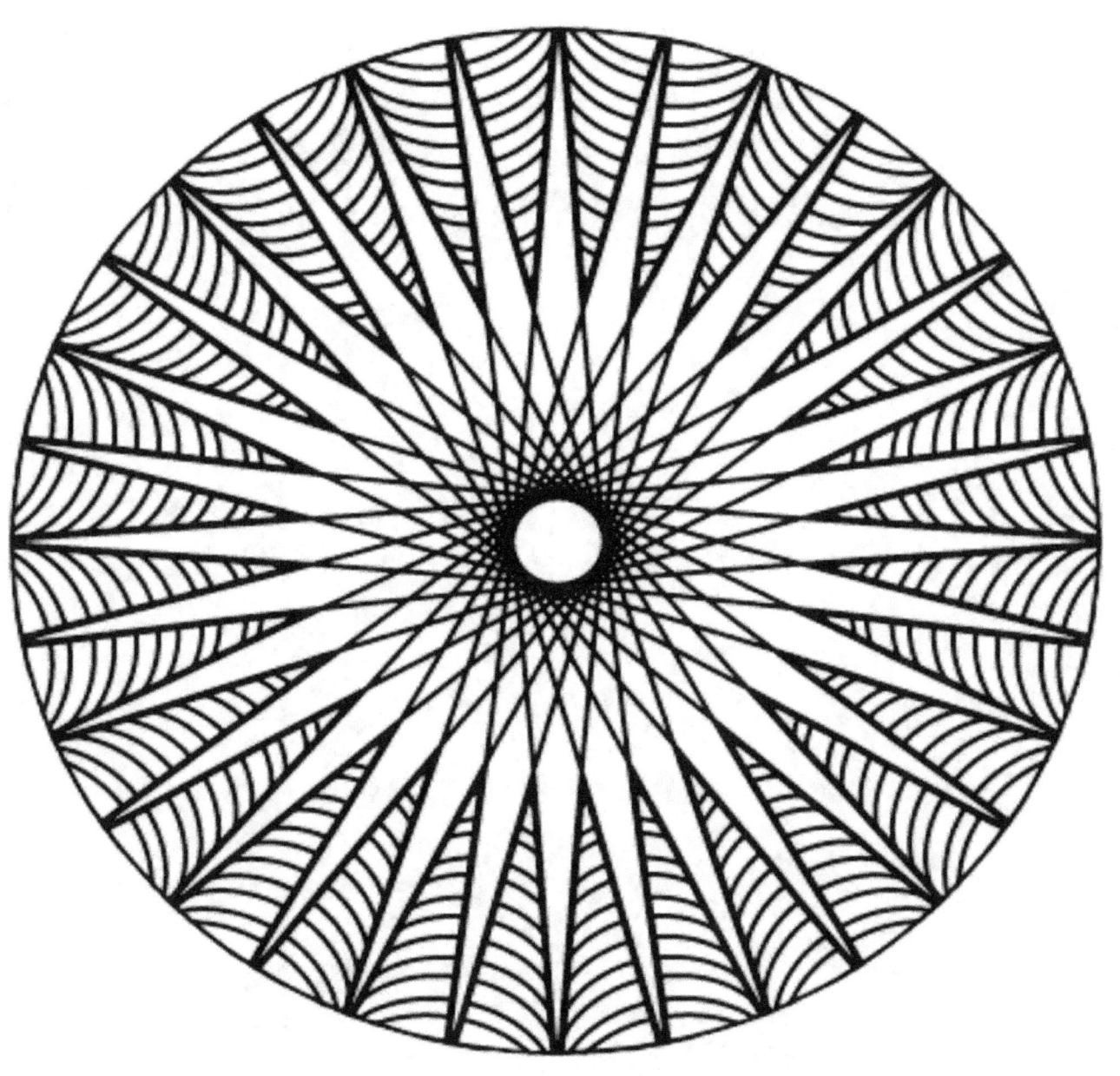

BLANK

PAGE

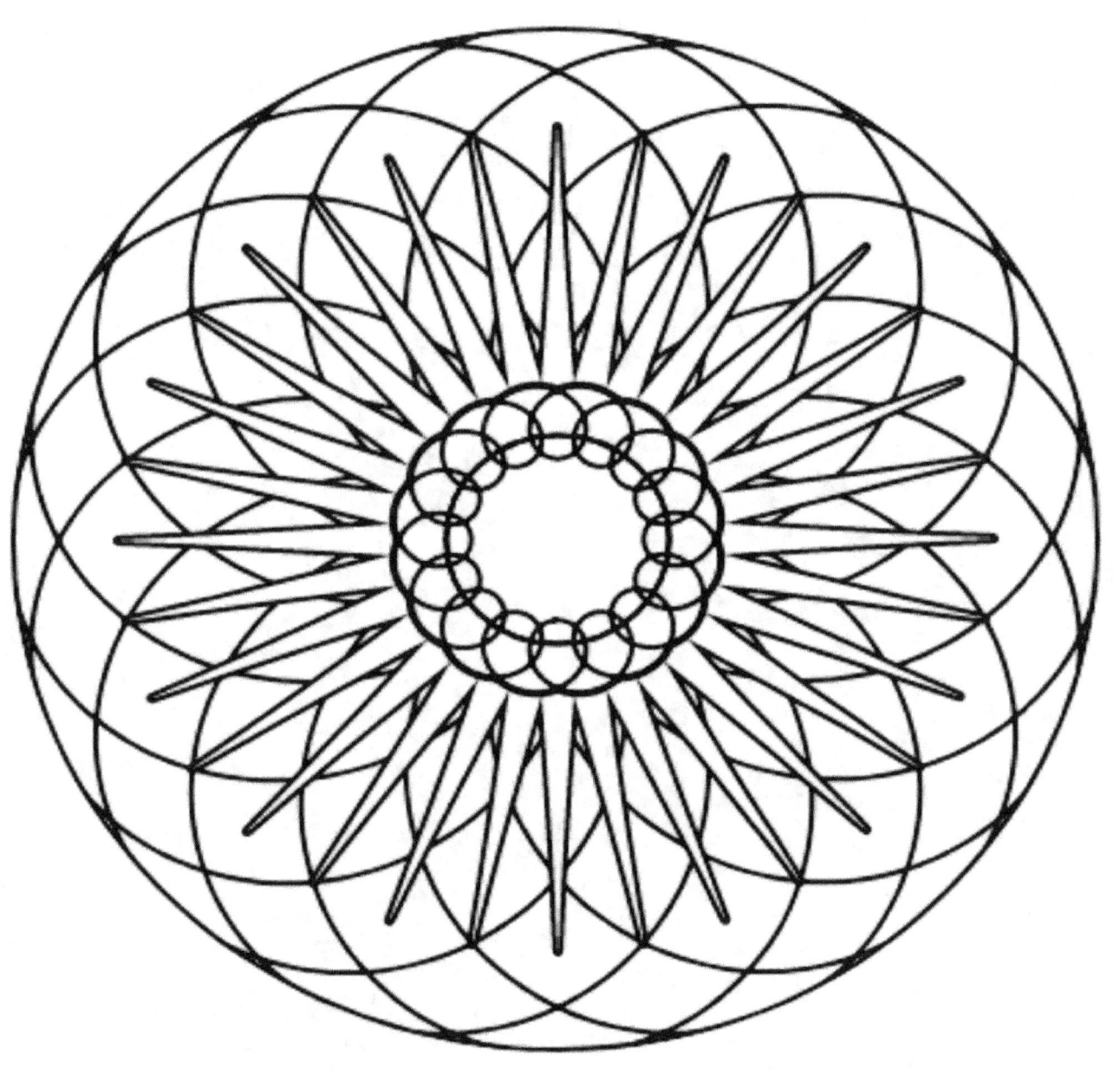

BLANK

PAGE

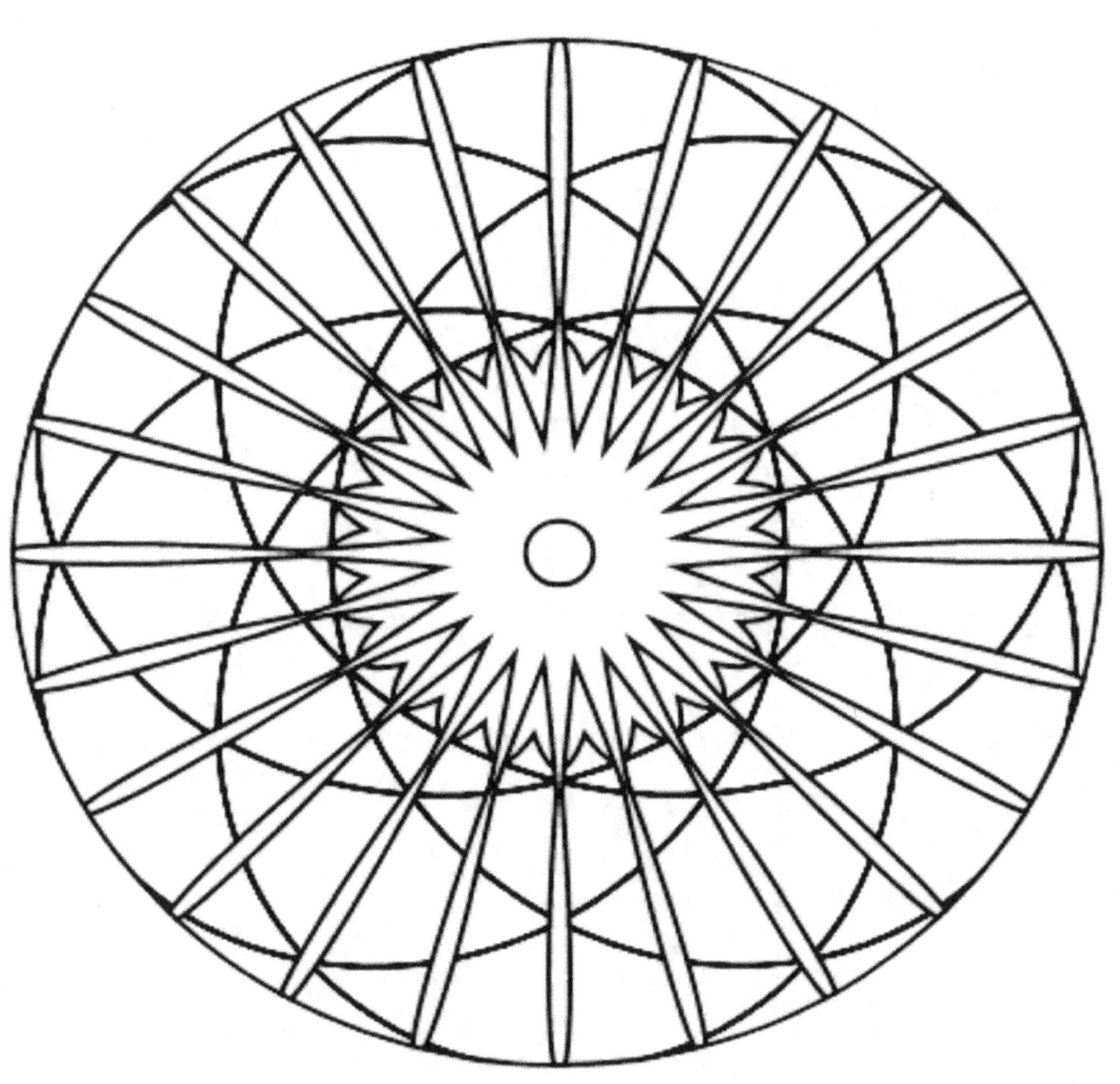

BLANK

PAGE

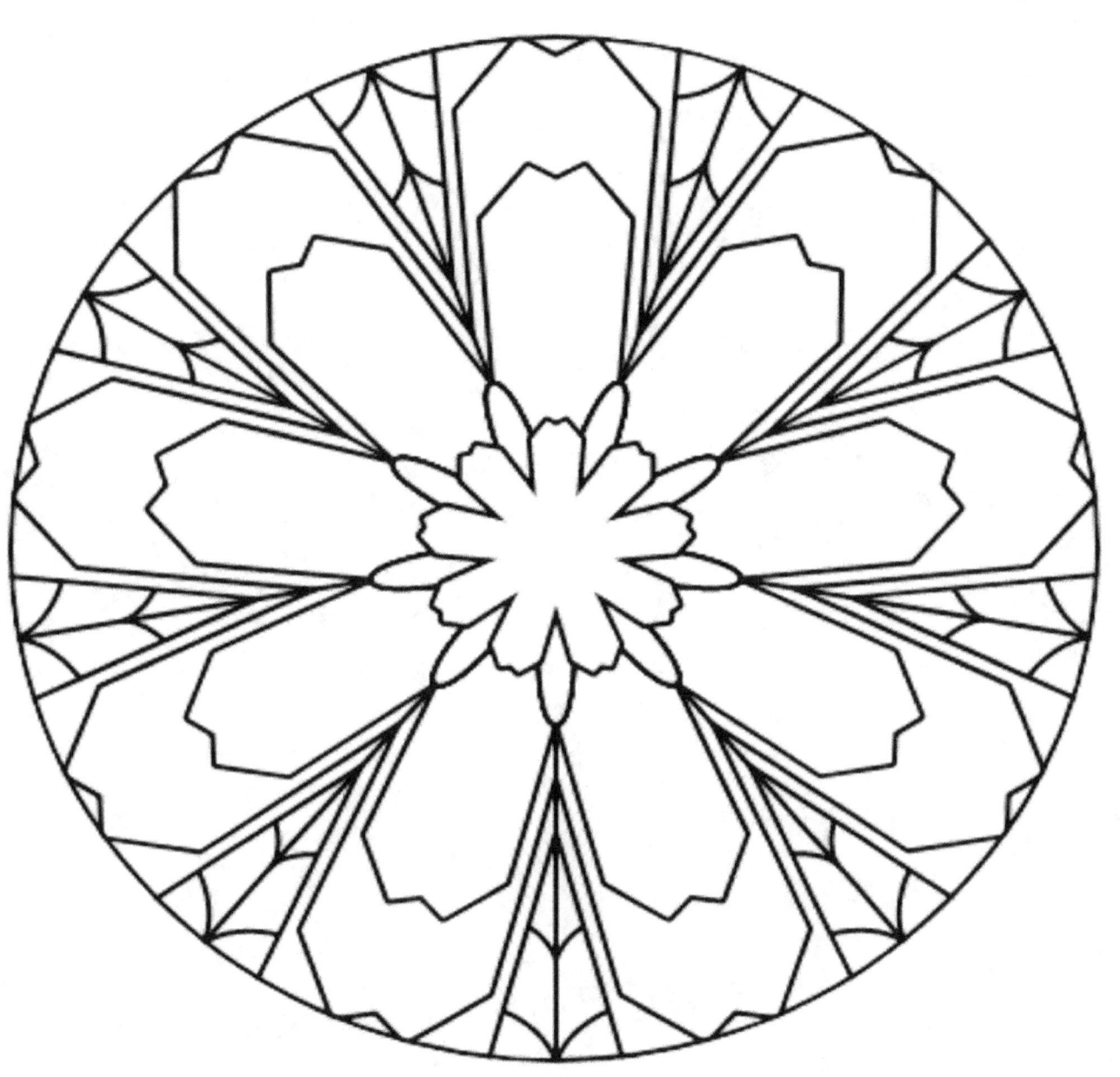

BLANK

PAGE

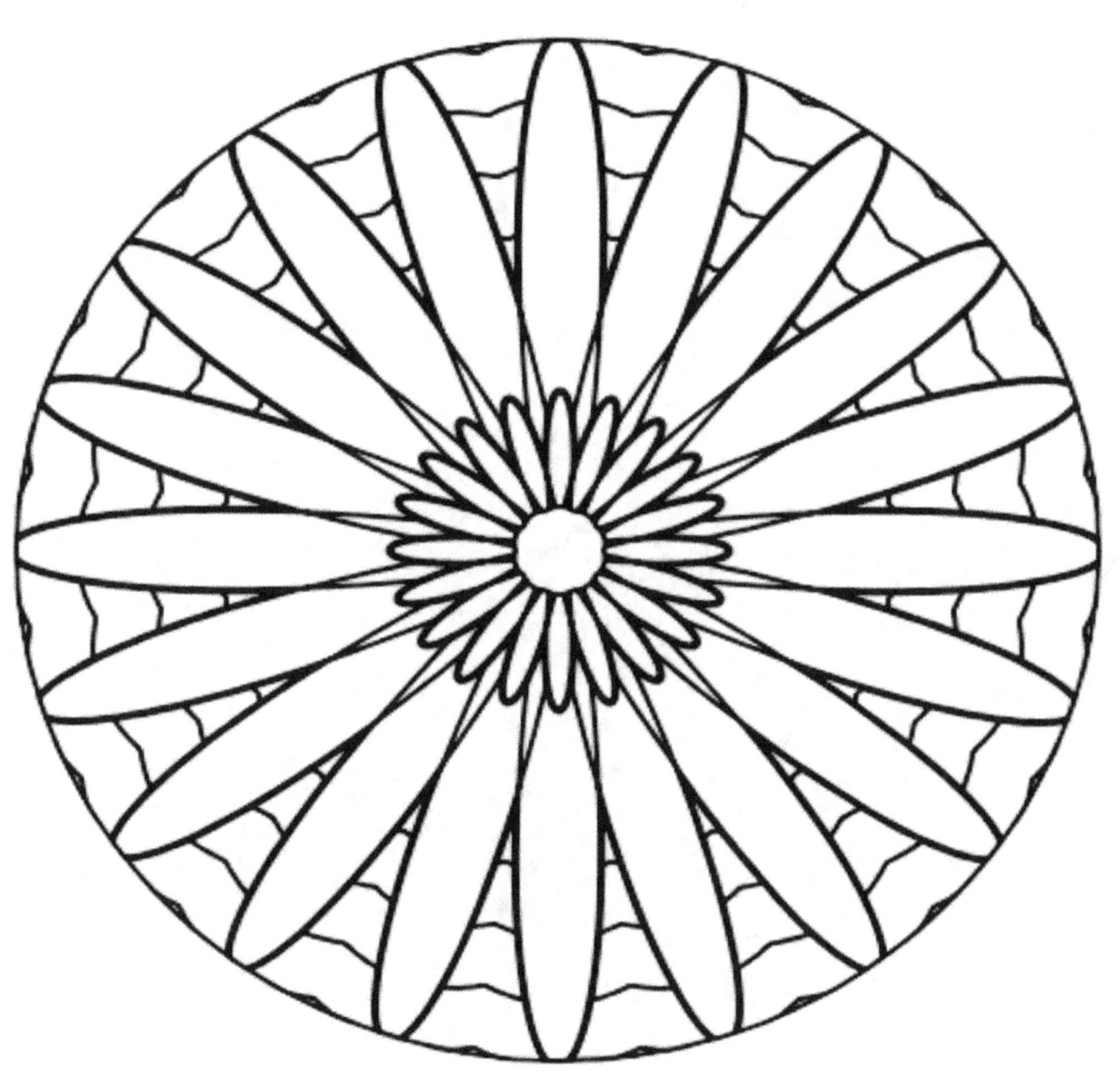

BLANK

PAGE

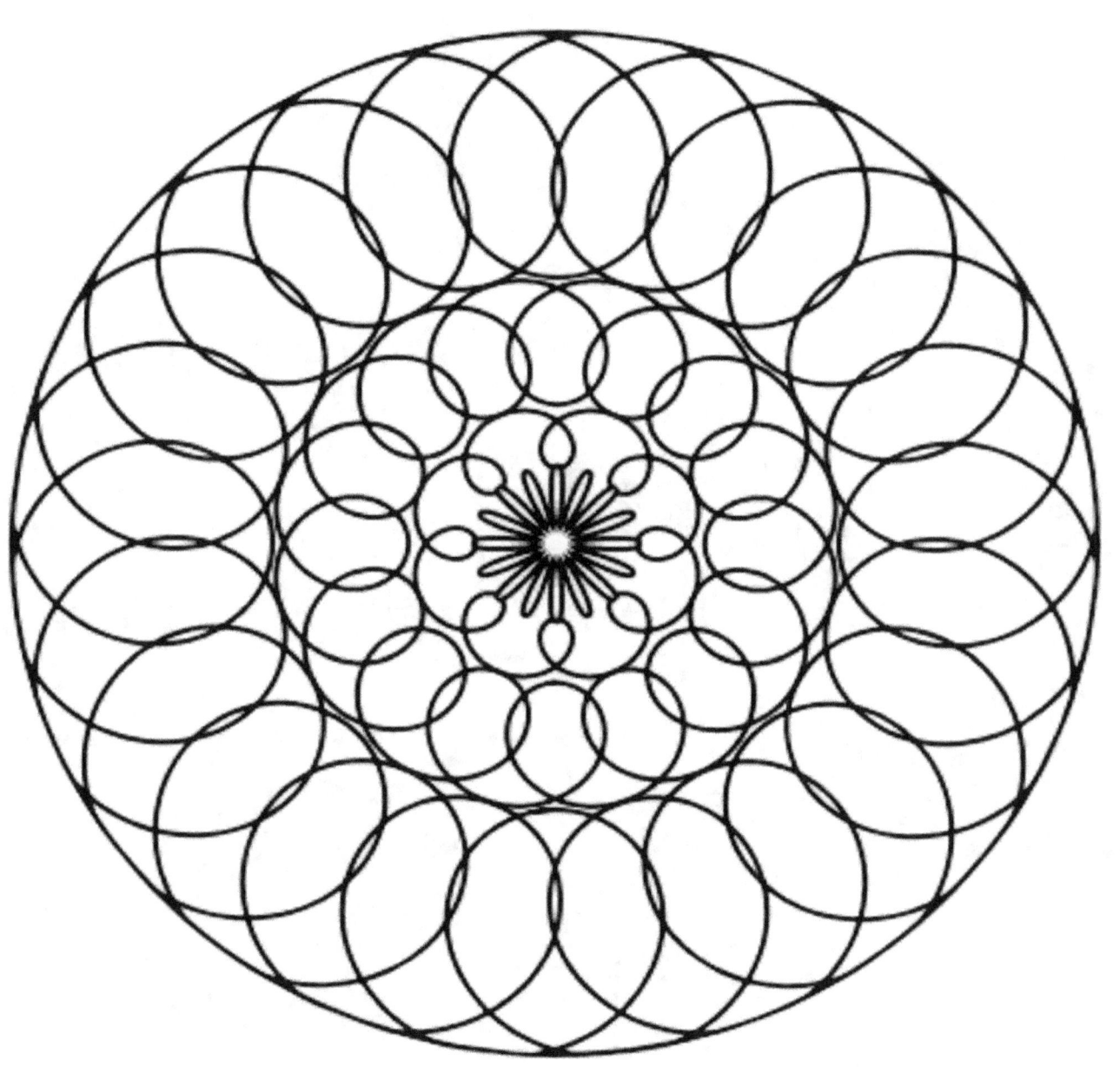

BLANK

PAGE

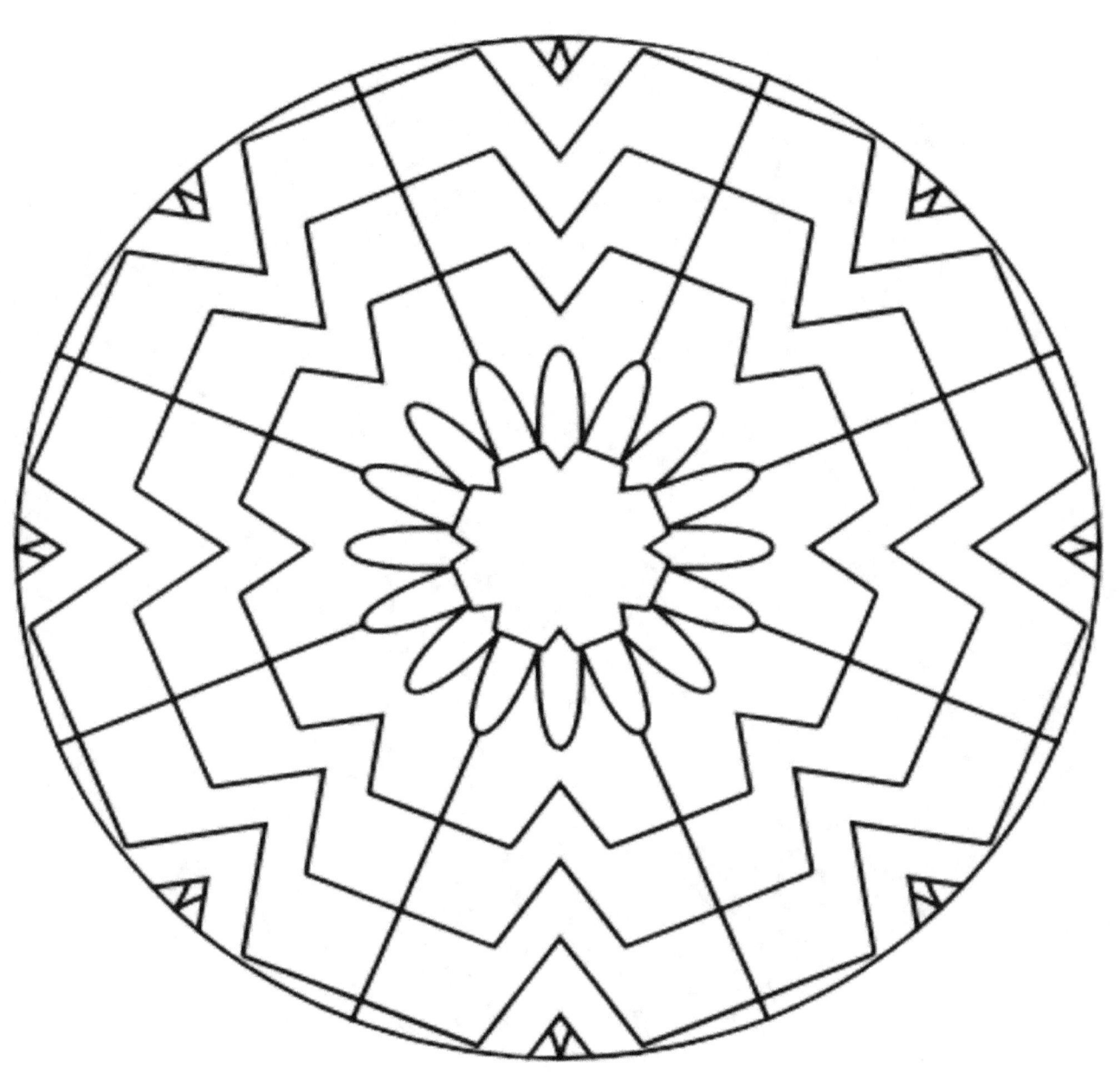

BLANK

PAGE

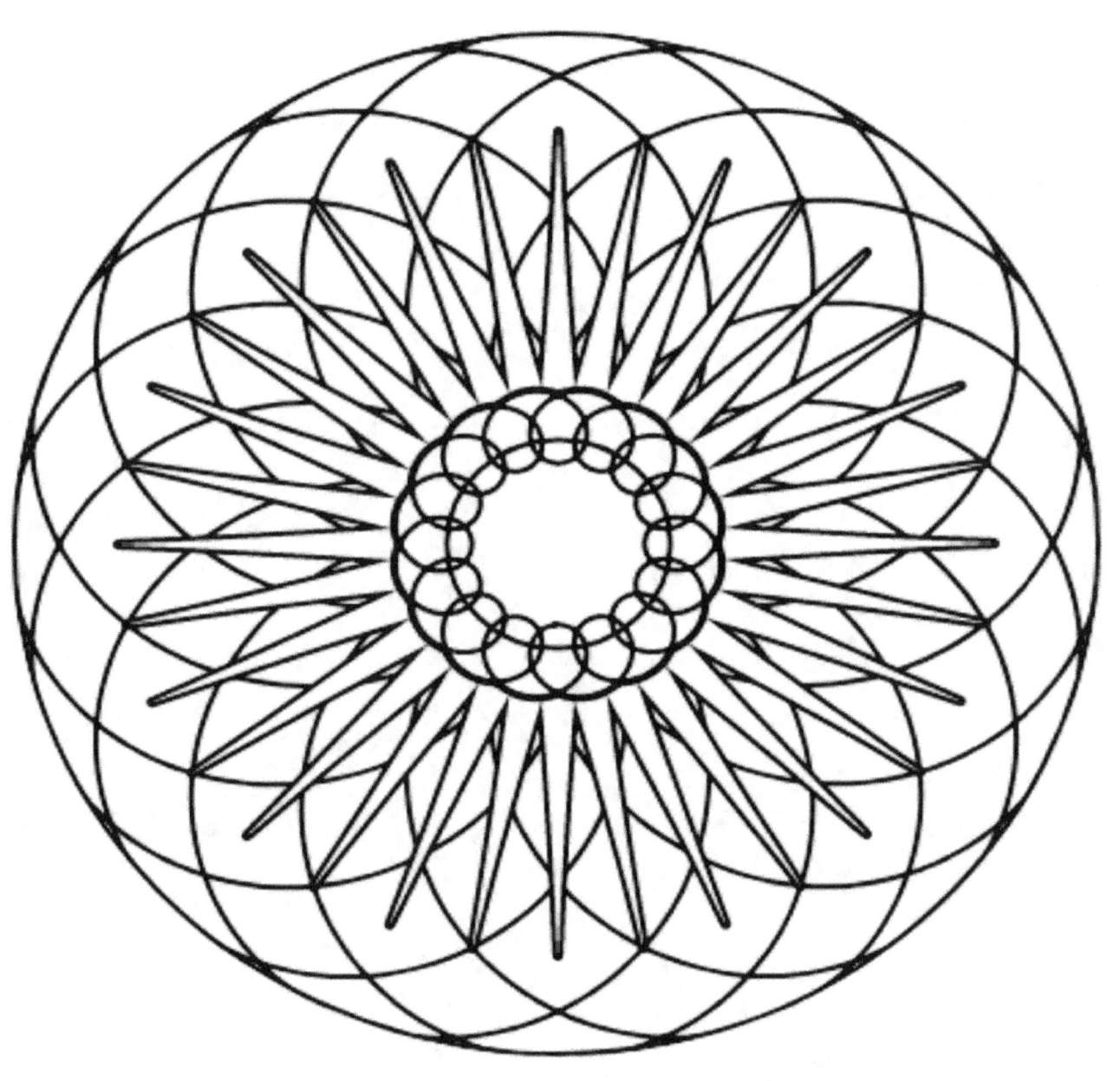

BLANK

PAGE

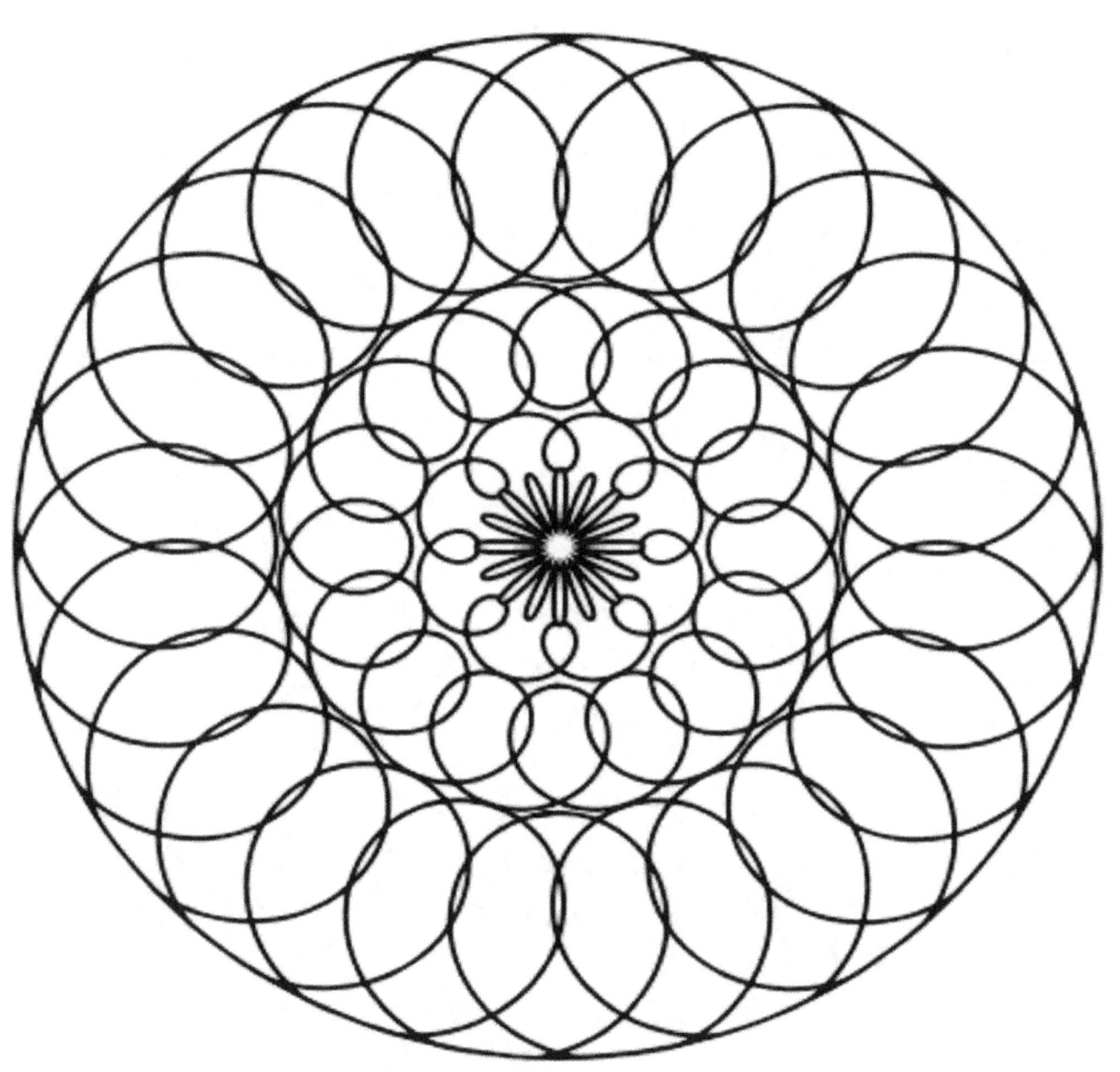

BLANK

PAGE

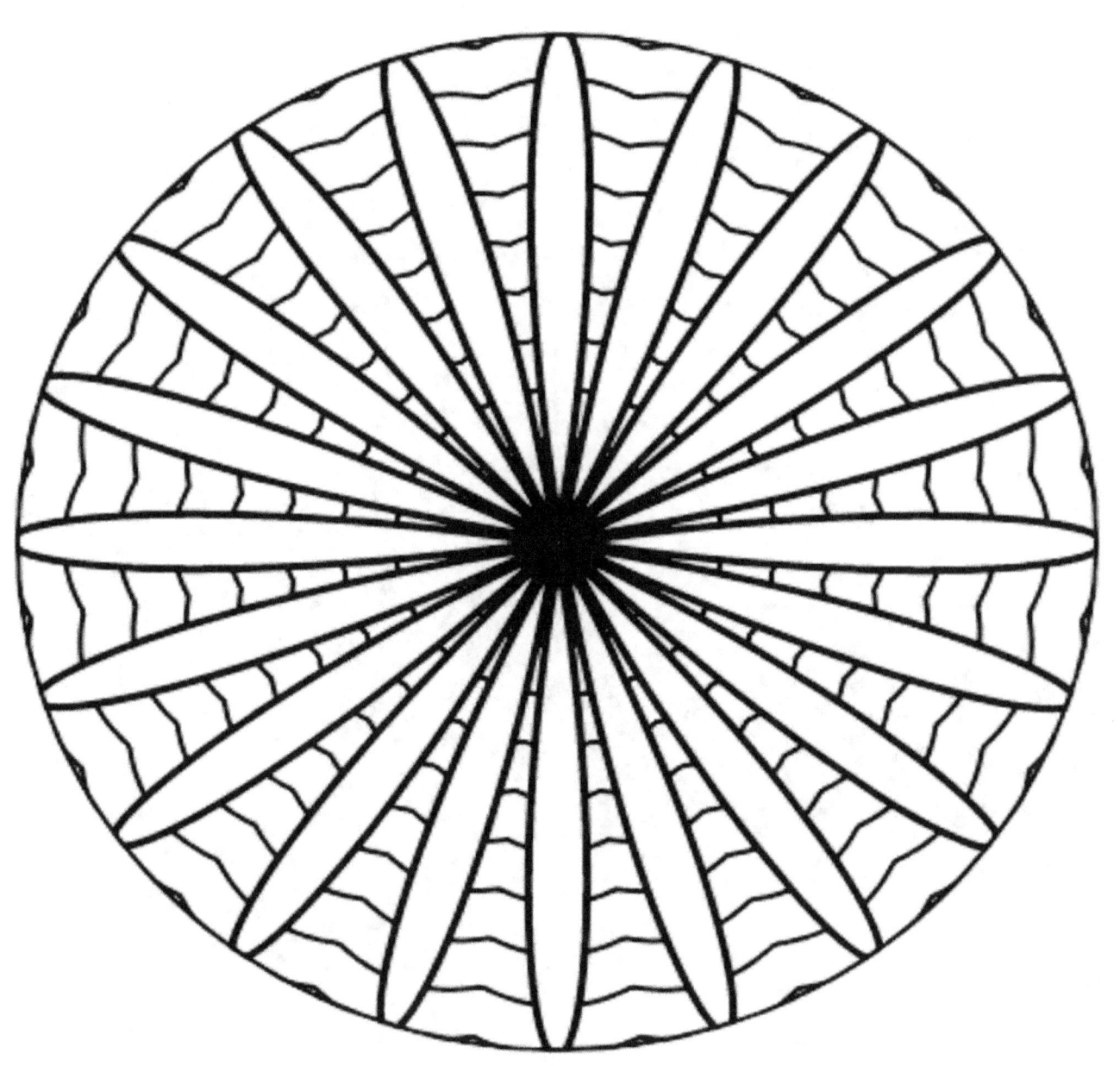

BLANK

PAGE

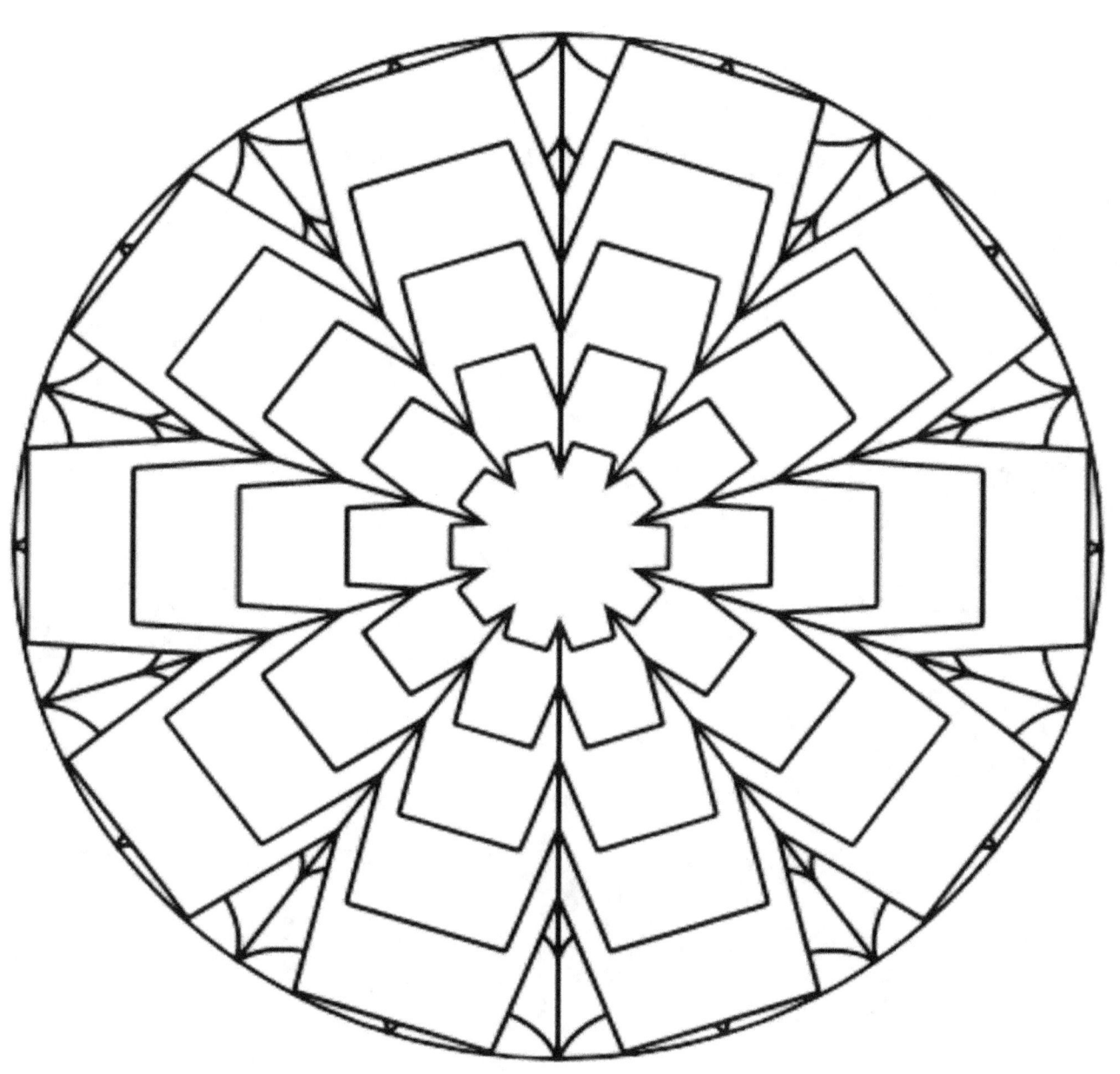

BLANK

PAGE

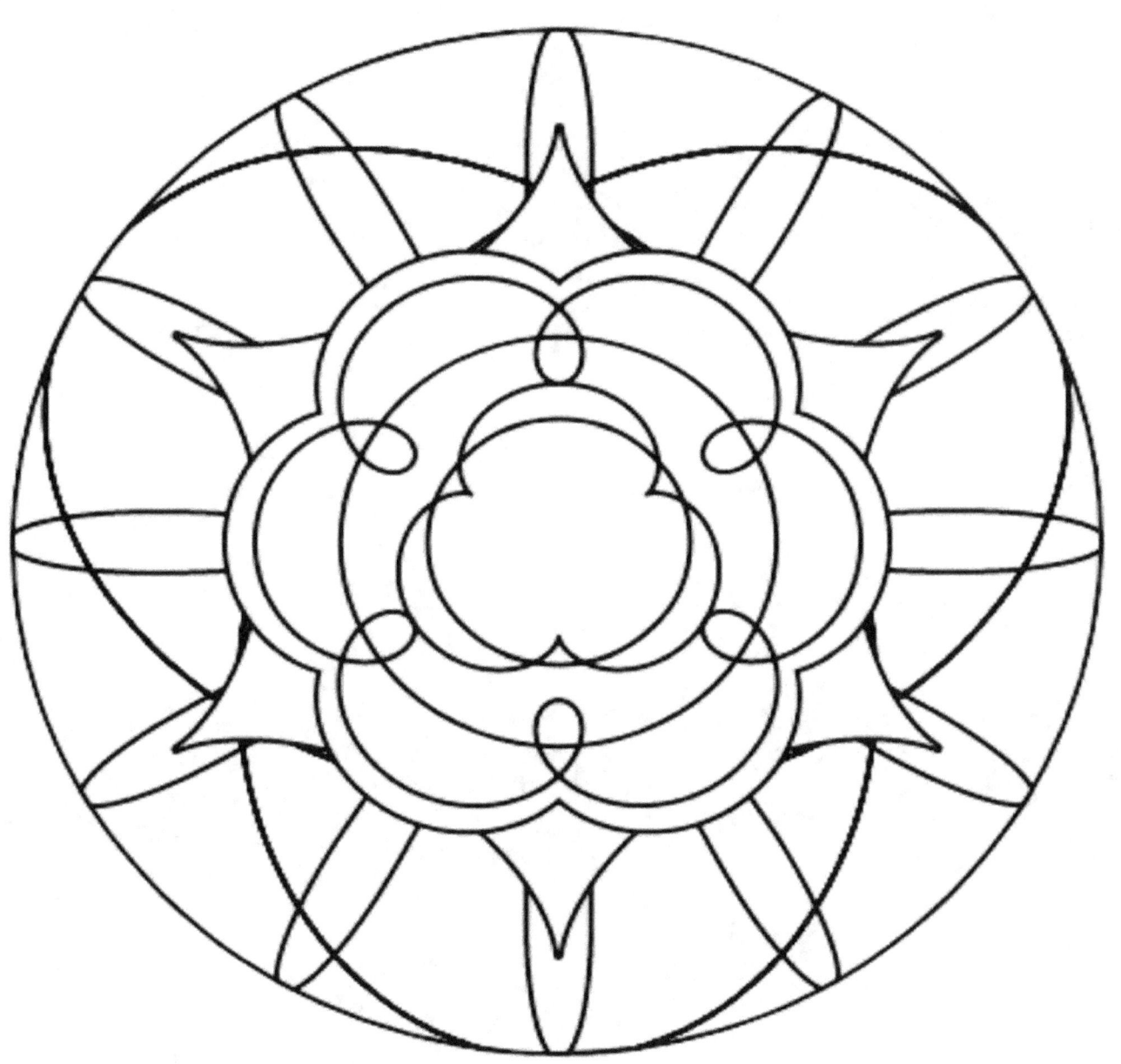

BLANK

PAGE